Hello!

my name is

I'm working from home

In my pajamas all day

Productive, I say

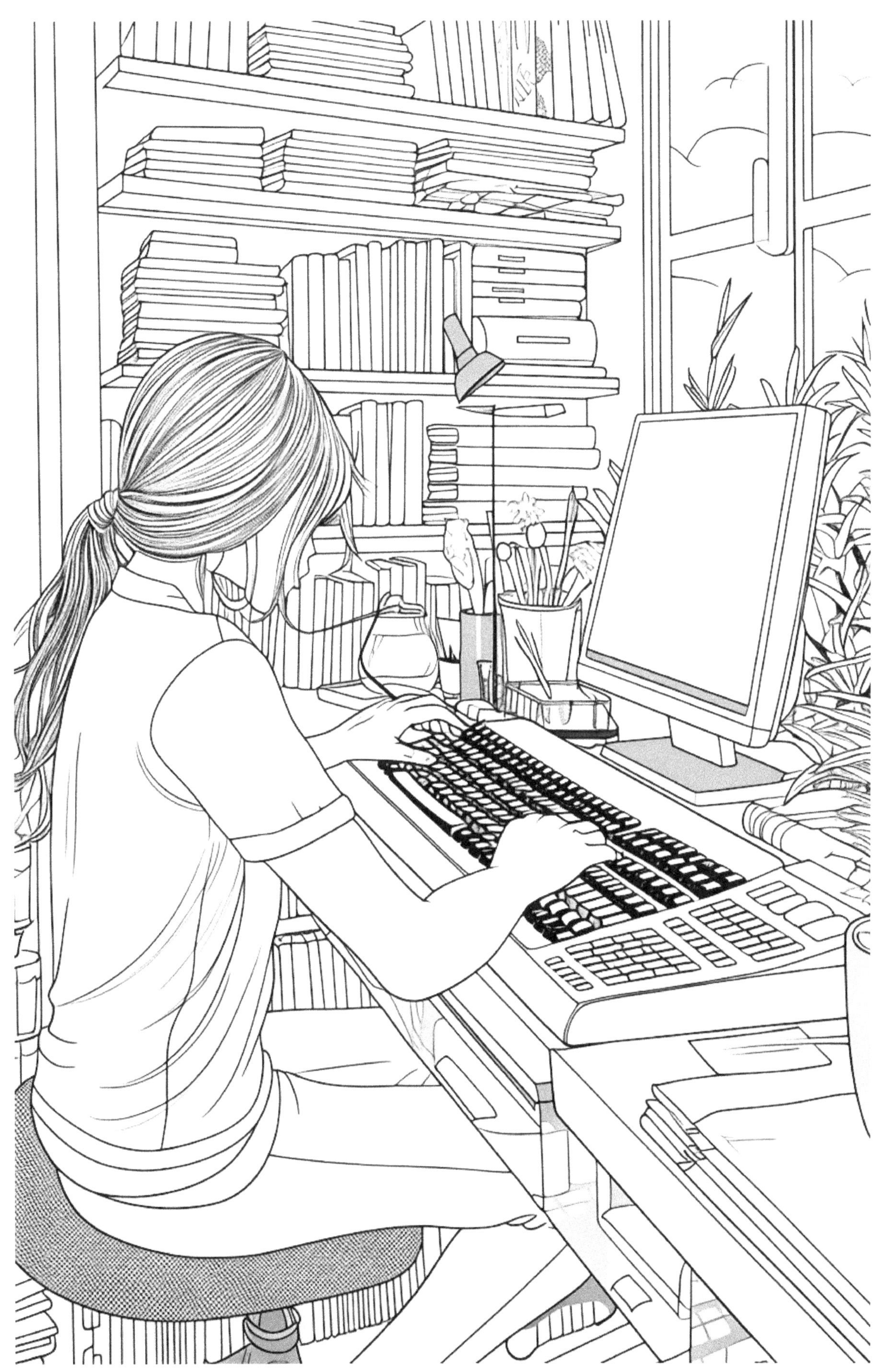

What to wear today?

A difficult decision

I will just wing it

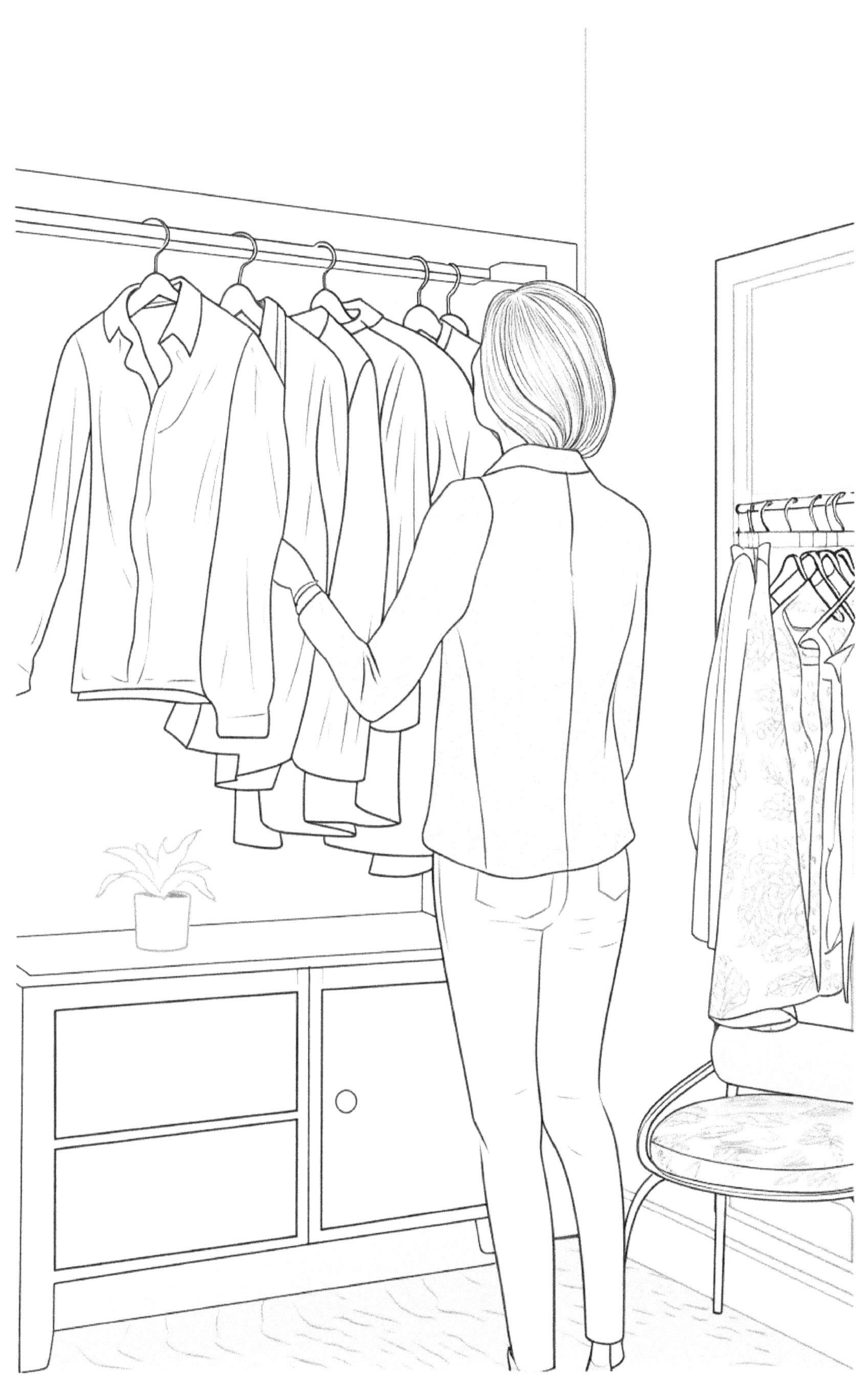

I'm washing my car

And suddenly a bird poops

Now I'm washing twice

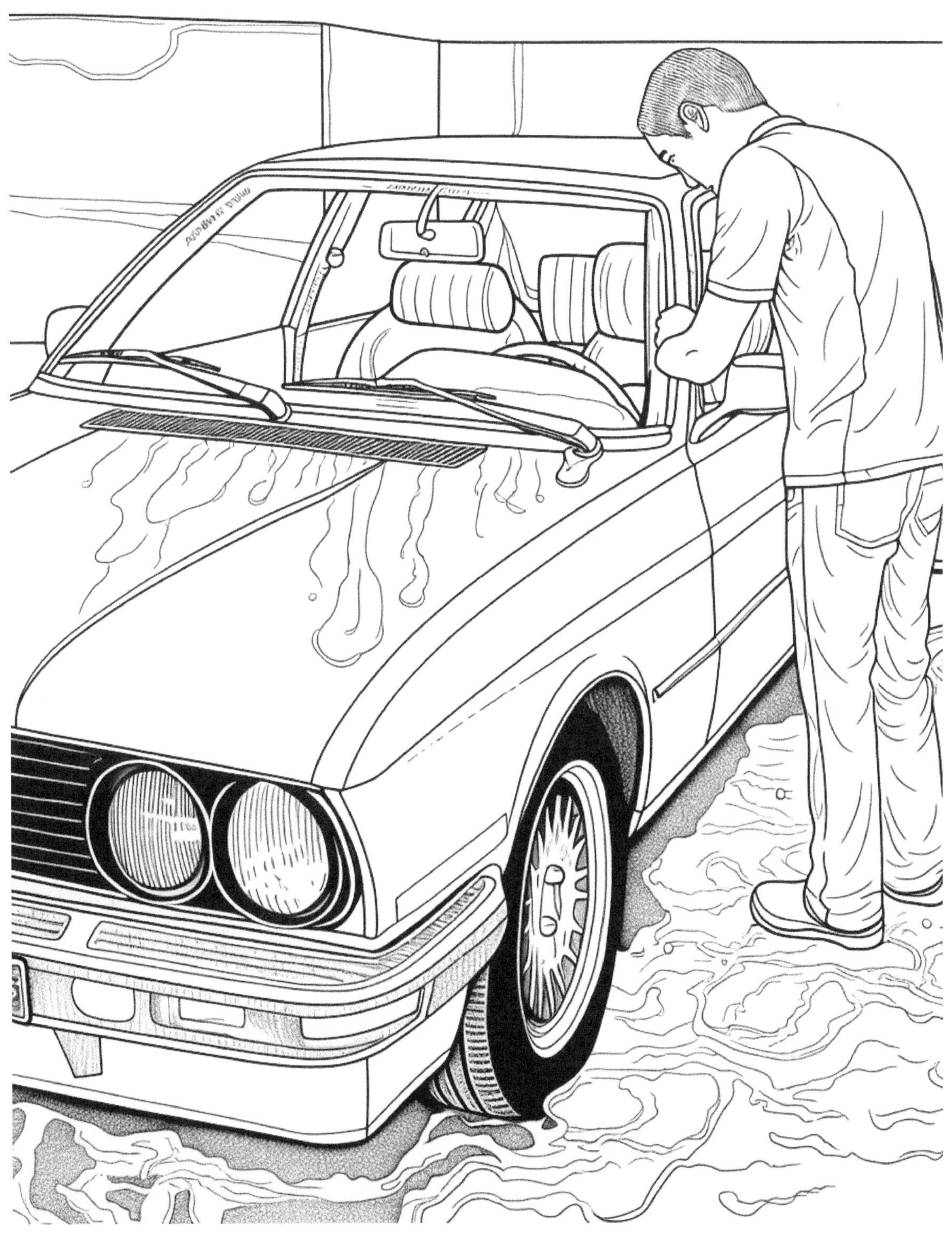

Coffee, oh coffee

How I wish I could vape you

Awakening blast

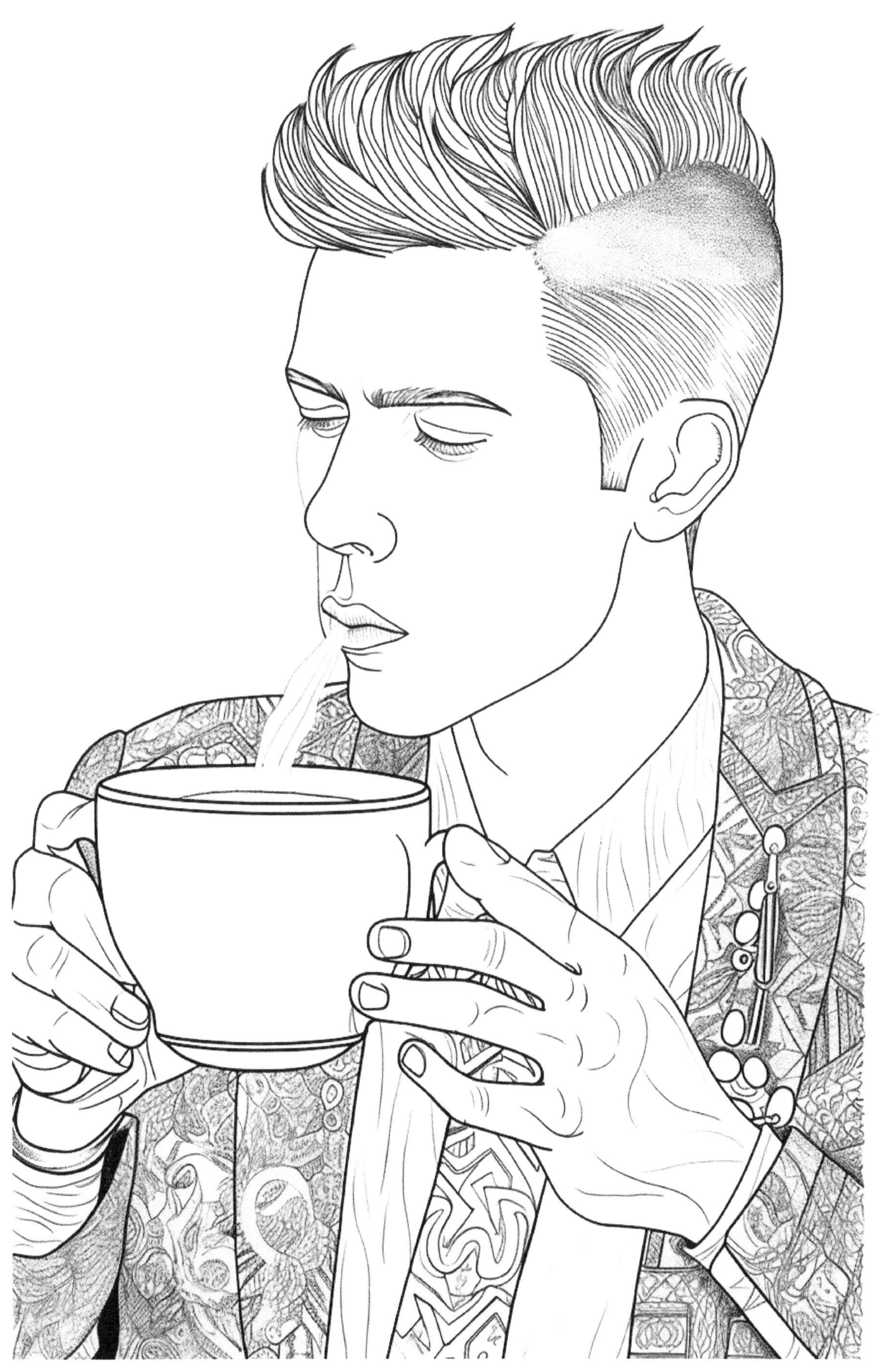

Printer, oh printer

Where do I put the paper?

It's a mystery

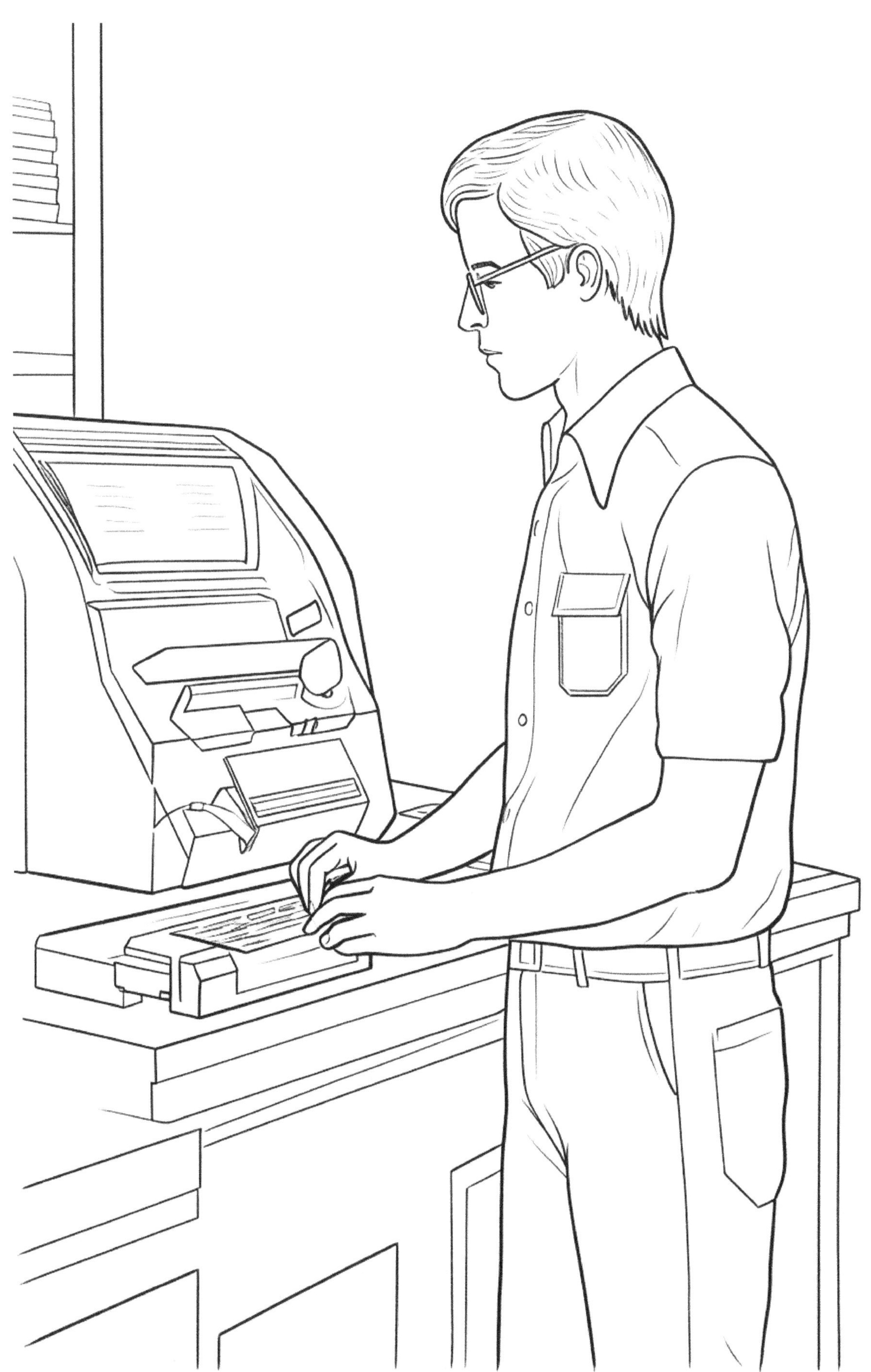

Tying shoes is hard

I'm a grown up, why can't I

Just wear those slip-ons?

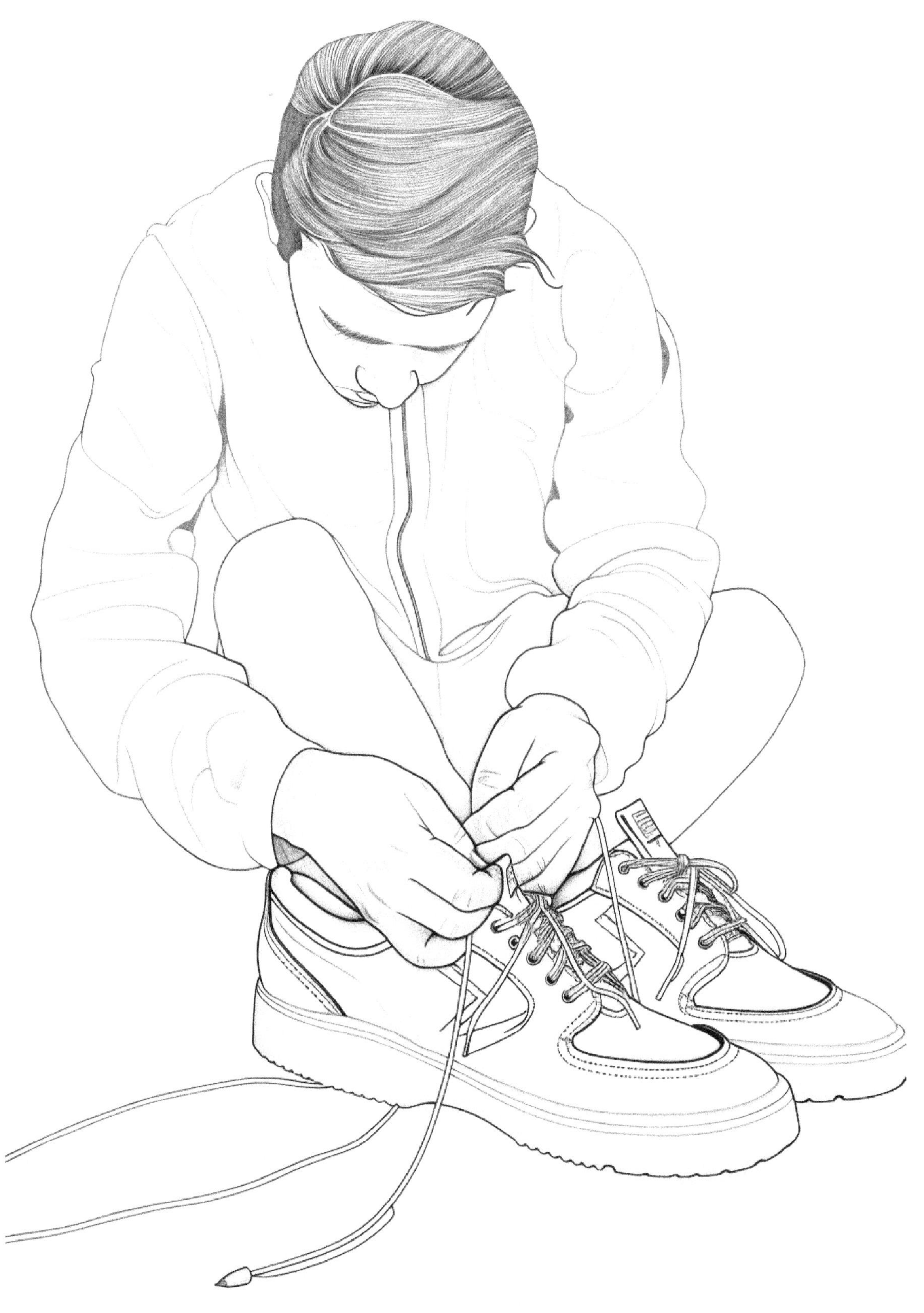

Trimming the bushes

I found a couple of gnomes

They were not happy

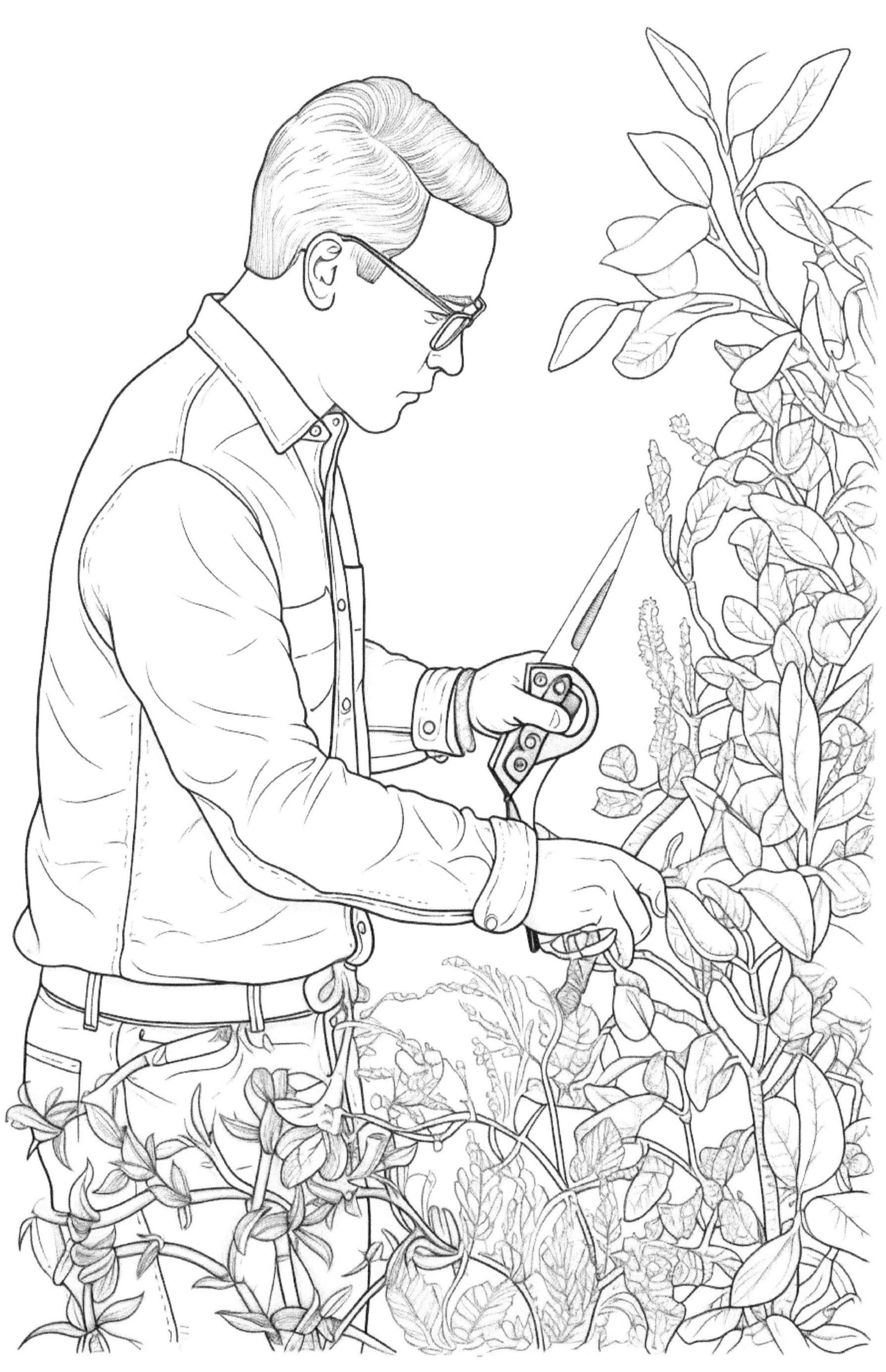

I bought too much stuff

Now I have to hide it all

From my wife and kid

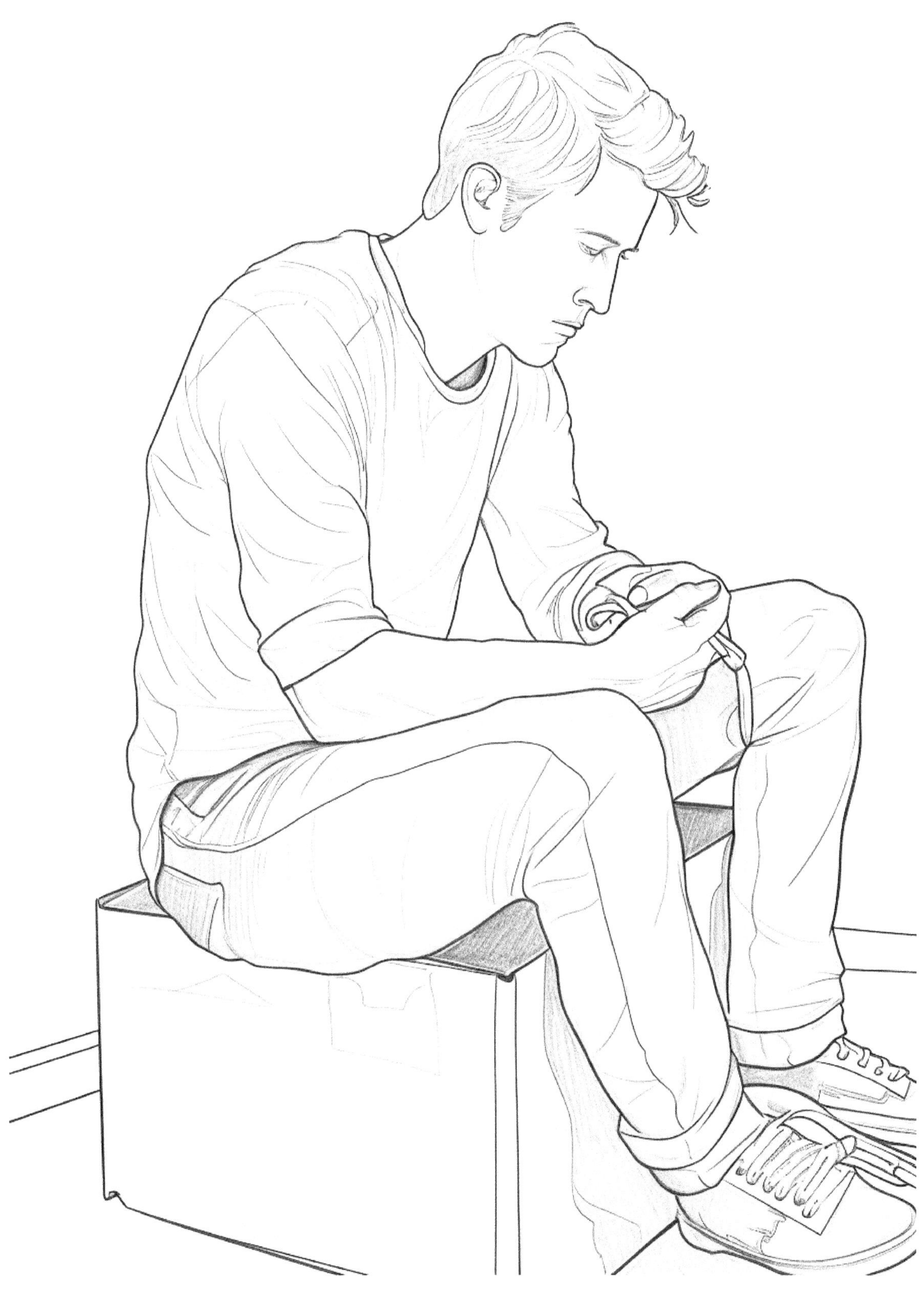

Swipe, swipe, swipe and swipe

I hope that I find someone

Who doesn't ghost me

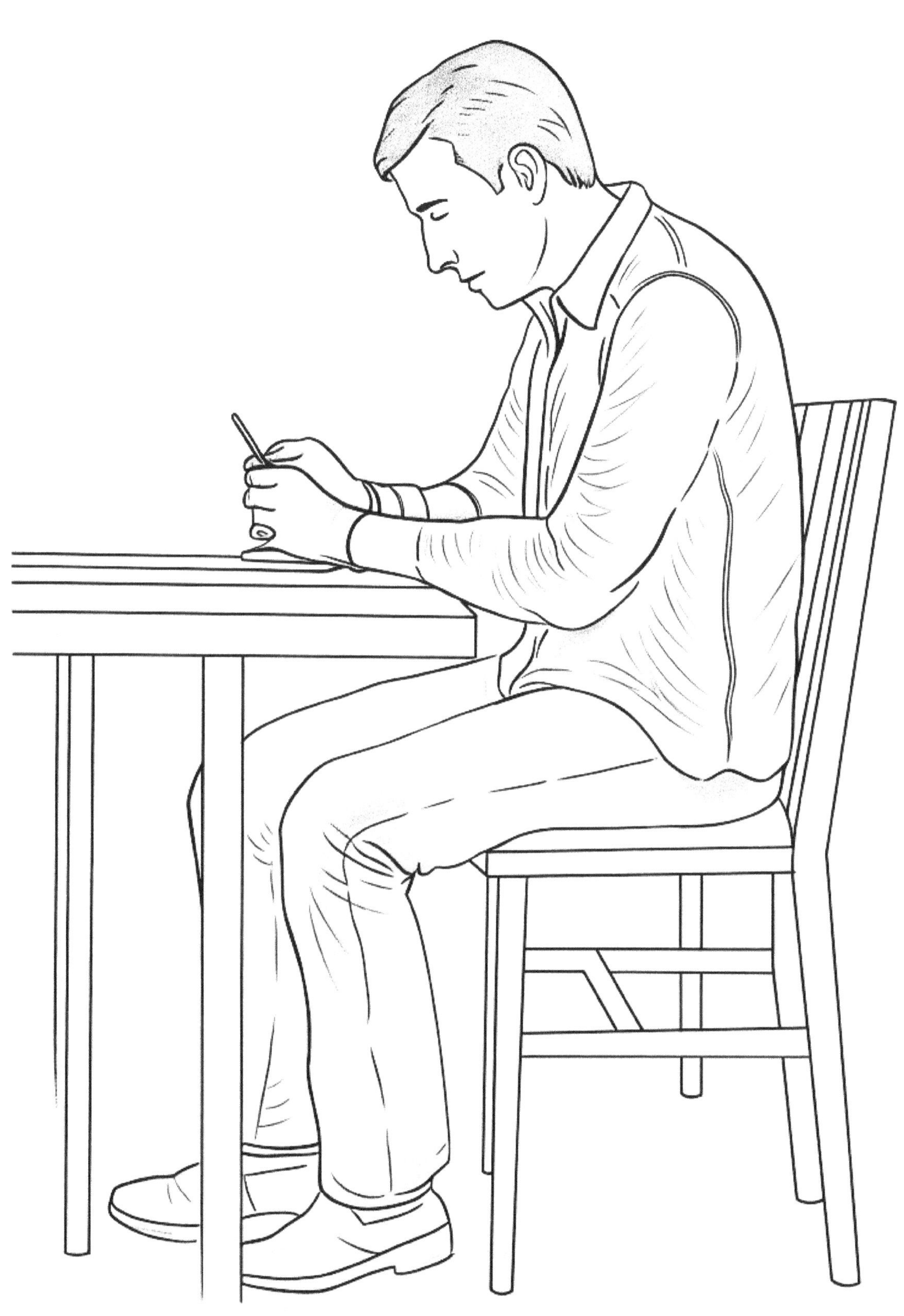

Bags are full of trash

I roll them out to the curb

And the neighbors stare

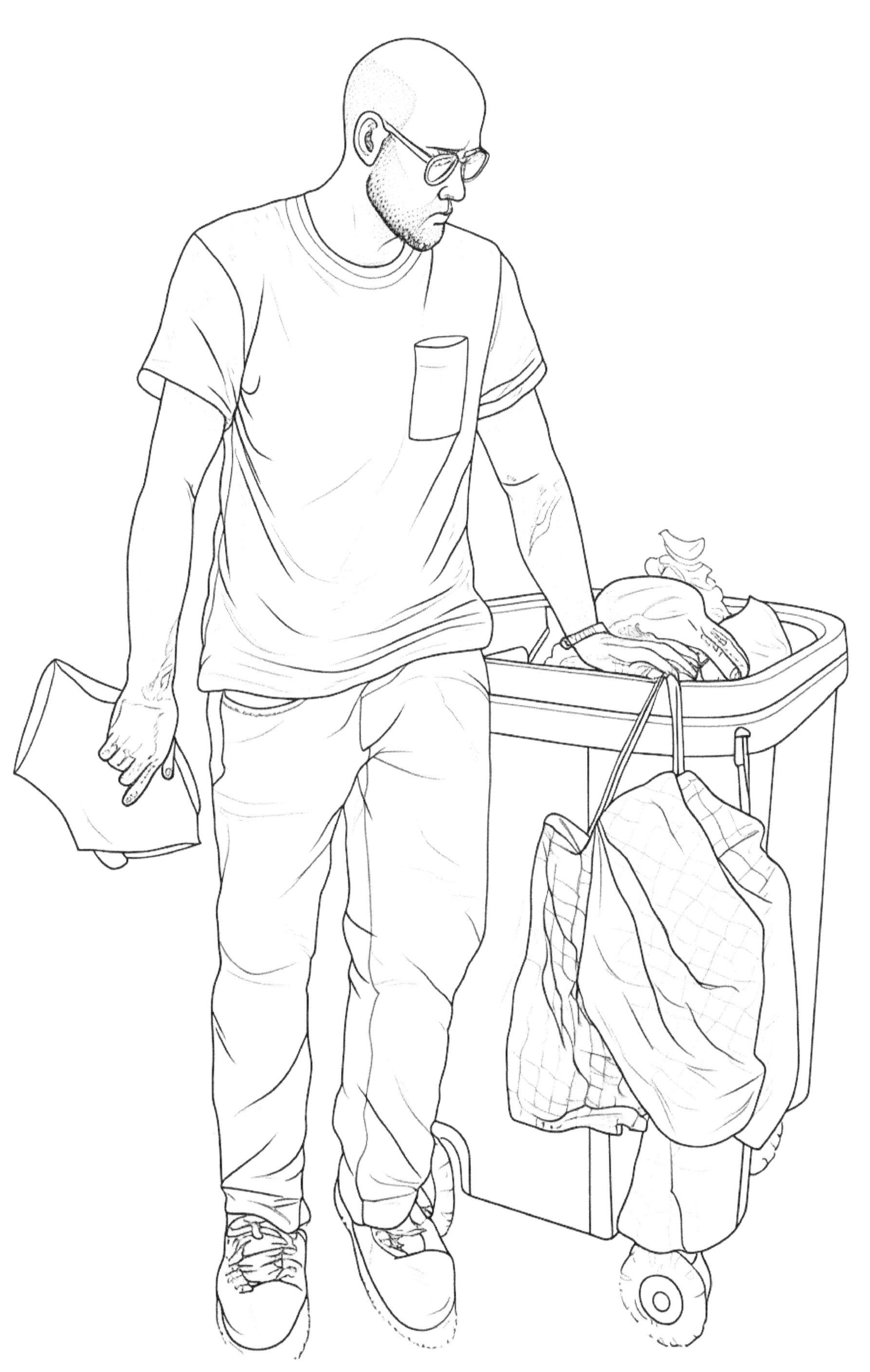

Scroll and scroll and scroll

So many cat videos

Help, I'm addicted

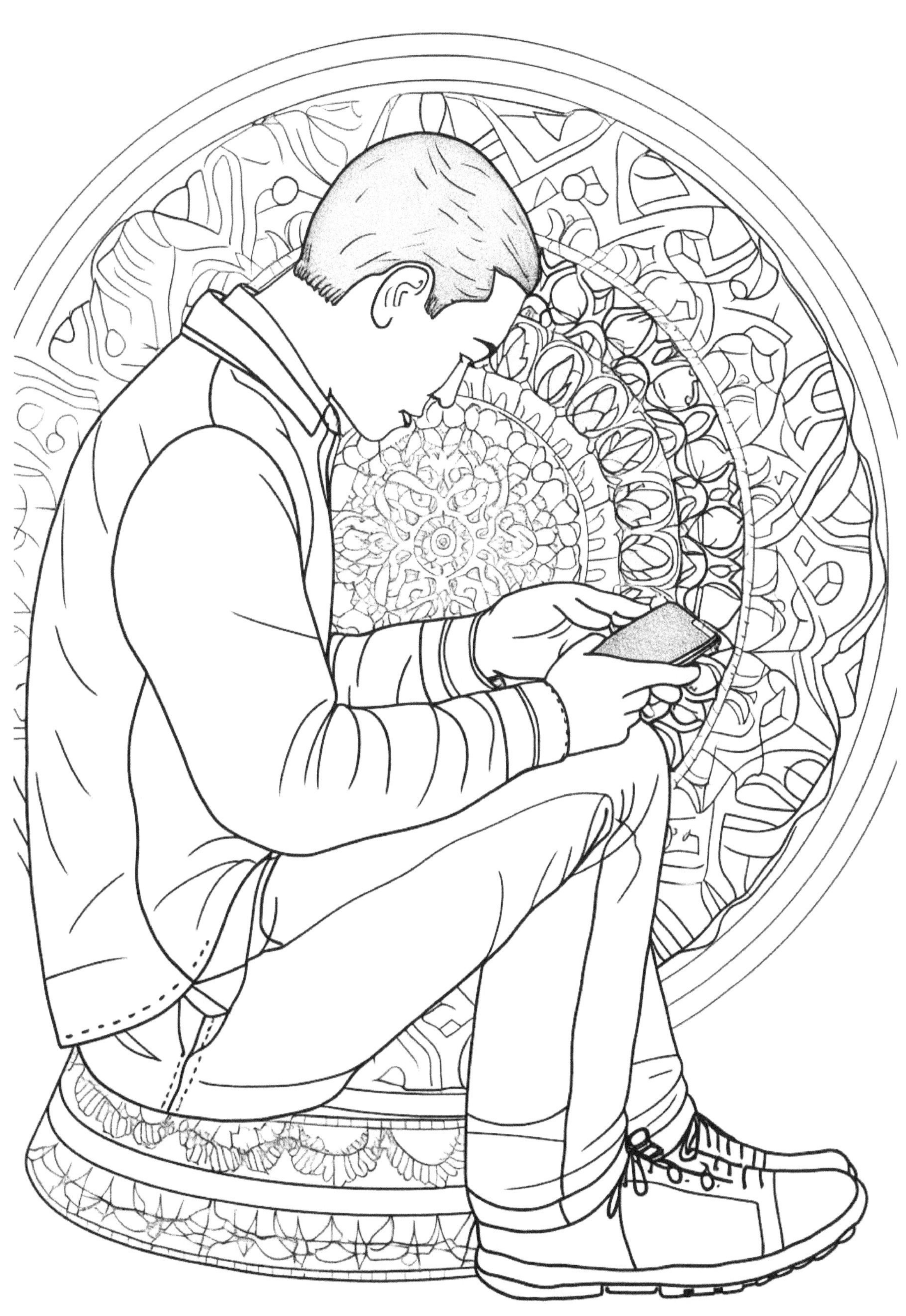

Alone in the park

I talk to the trees and birds

They are my friends now

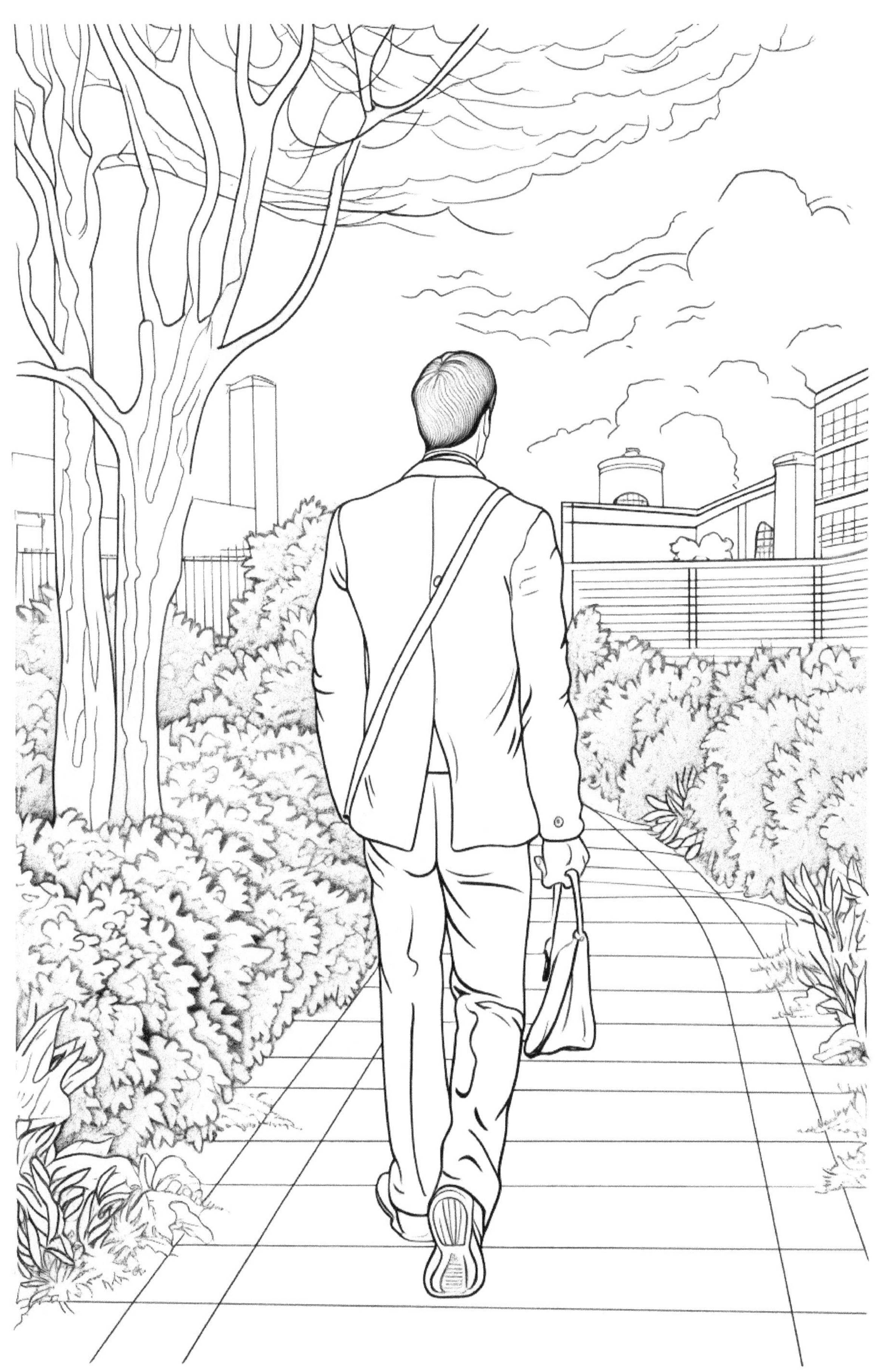

The news is a mess

So I'll just read the headlines

And pretend I know

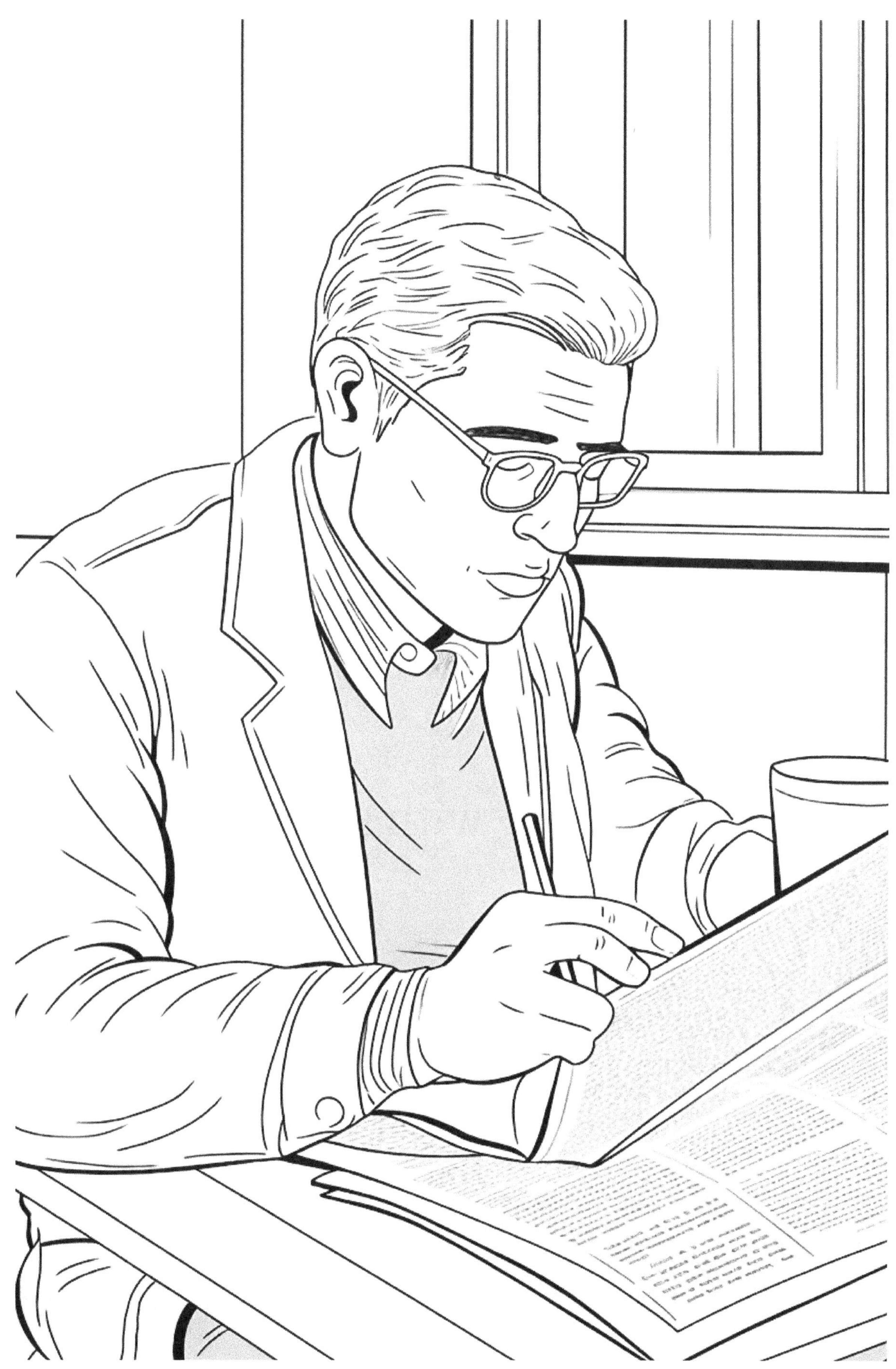

Shopping cart walkers

We are the new breed of old

Aging with style

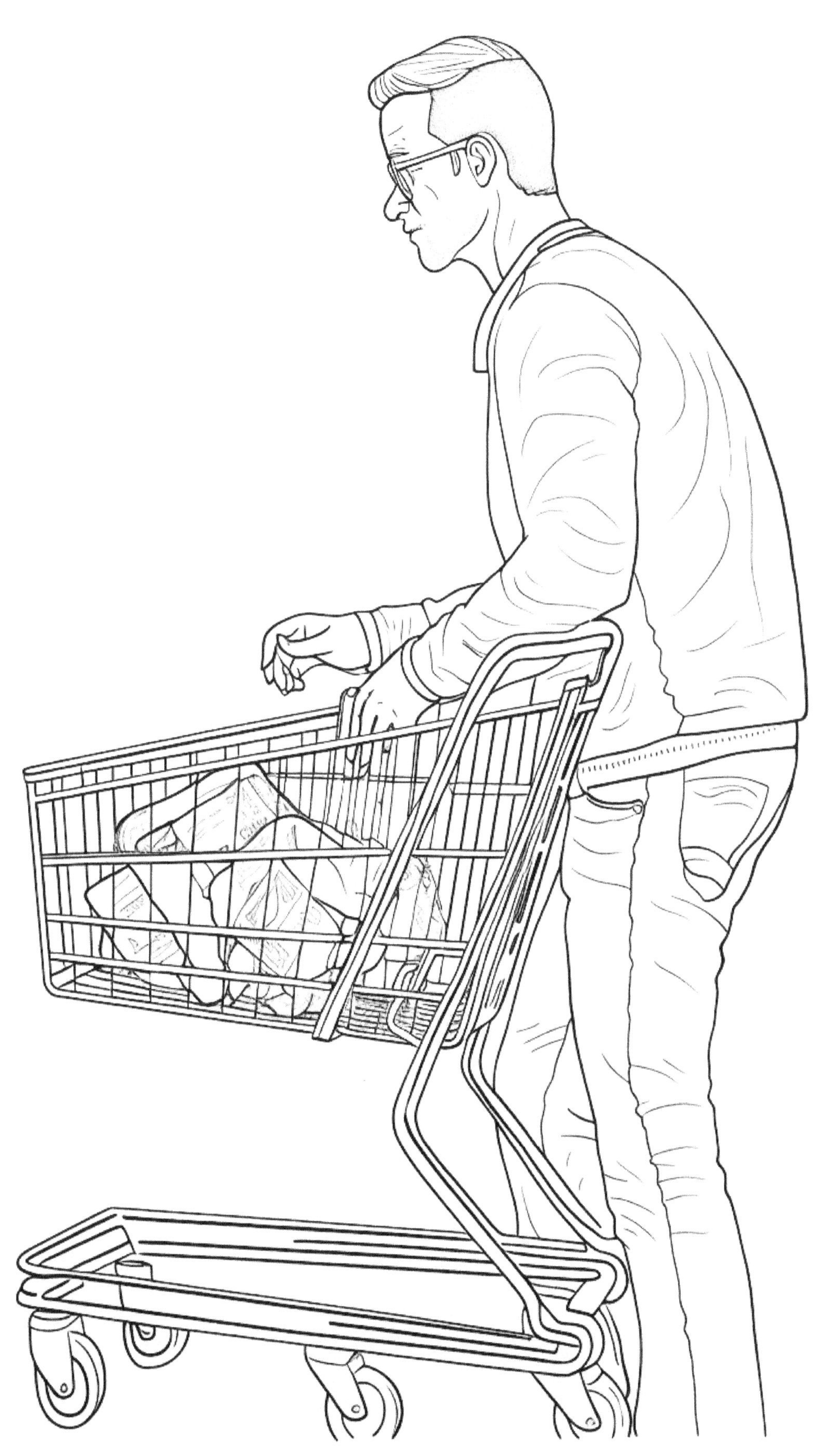

Shirt buttons, so small

Battle of patience and will

I might just give up

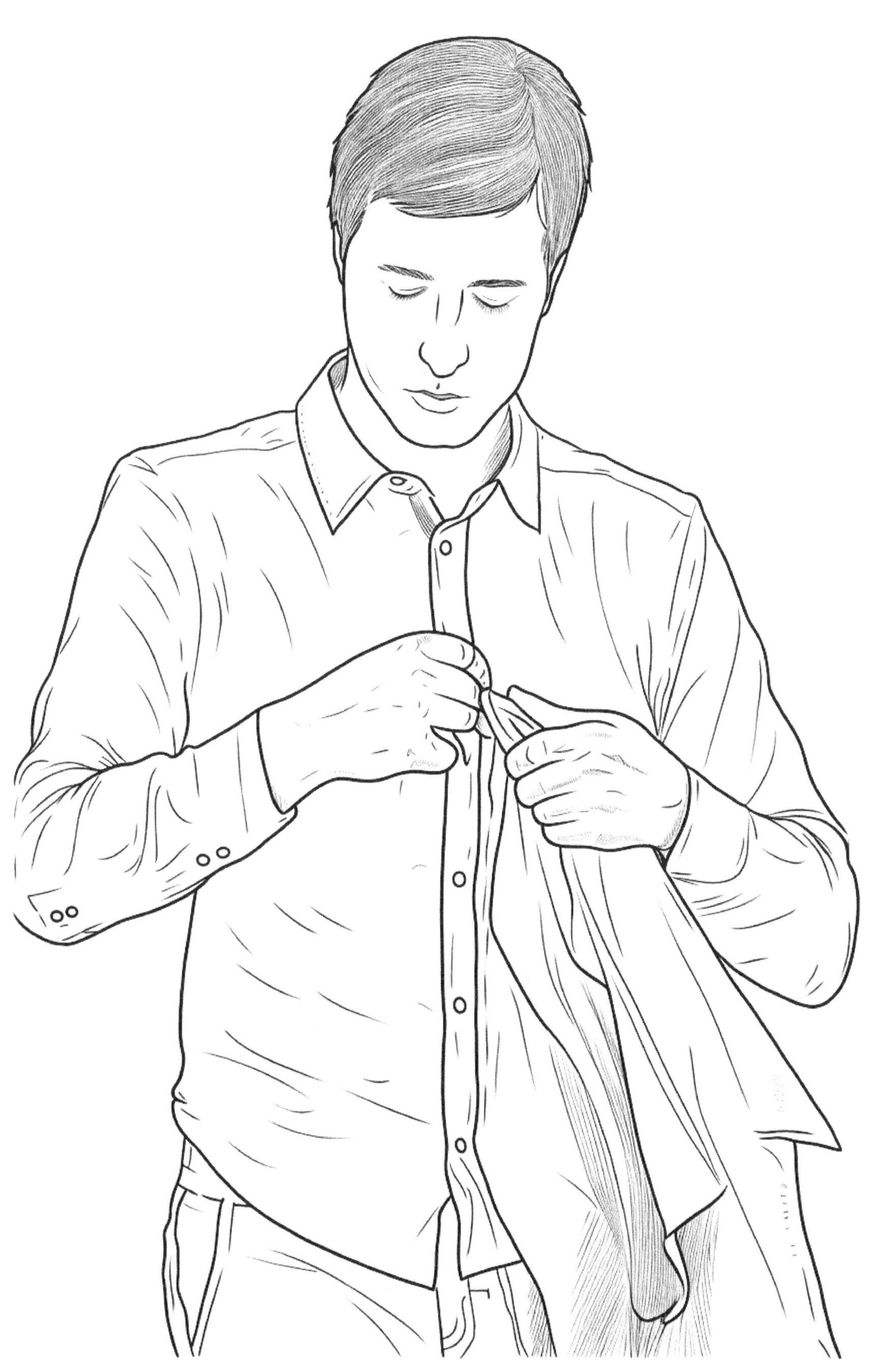

Pumpkin spice latte

A fall drink that tastes like home

Warms me from inside

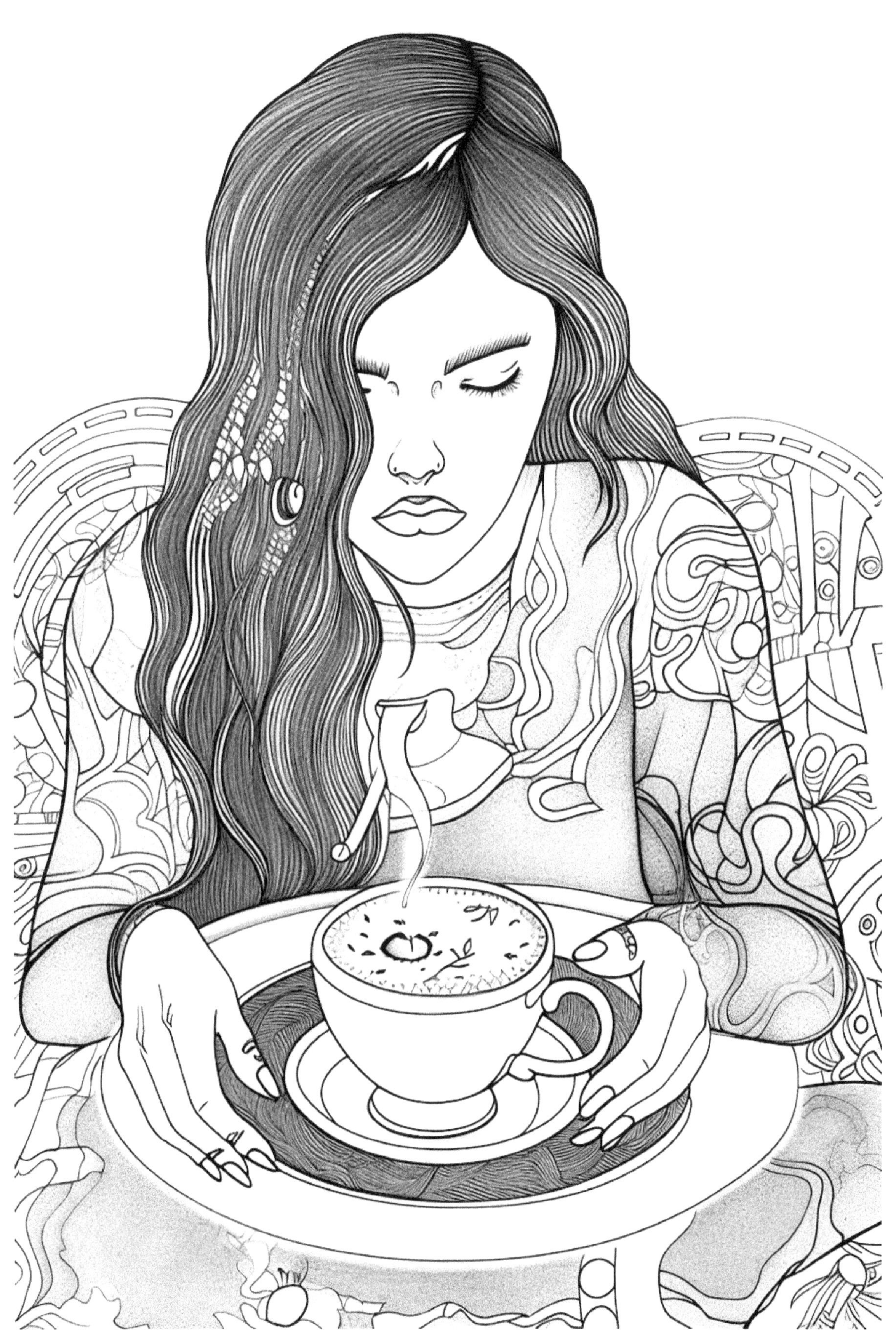

Weeds, oh weeds, you're pests

But your roots make good compost

So thanks for the help

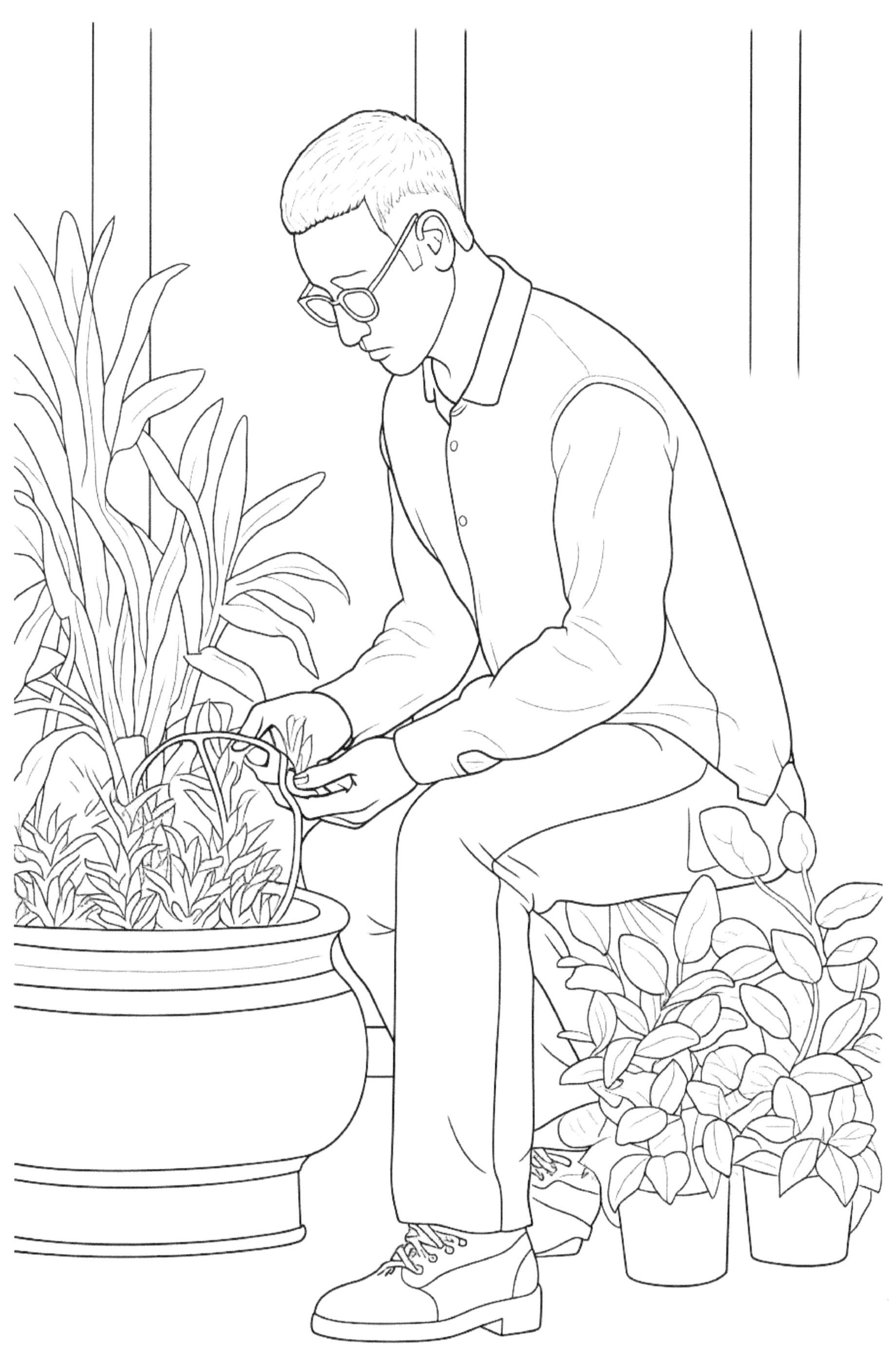

Great equalizer

That's public transportation

Trying to arrive

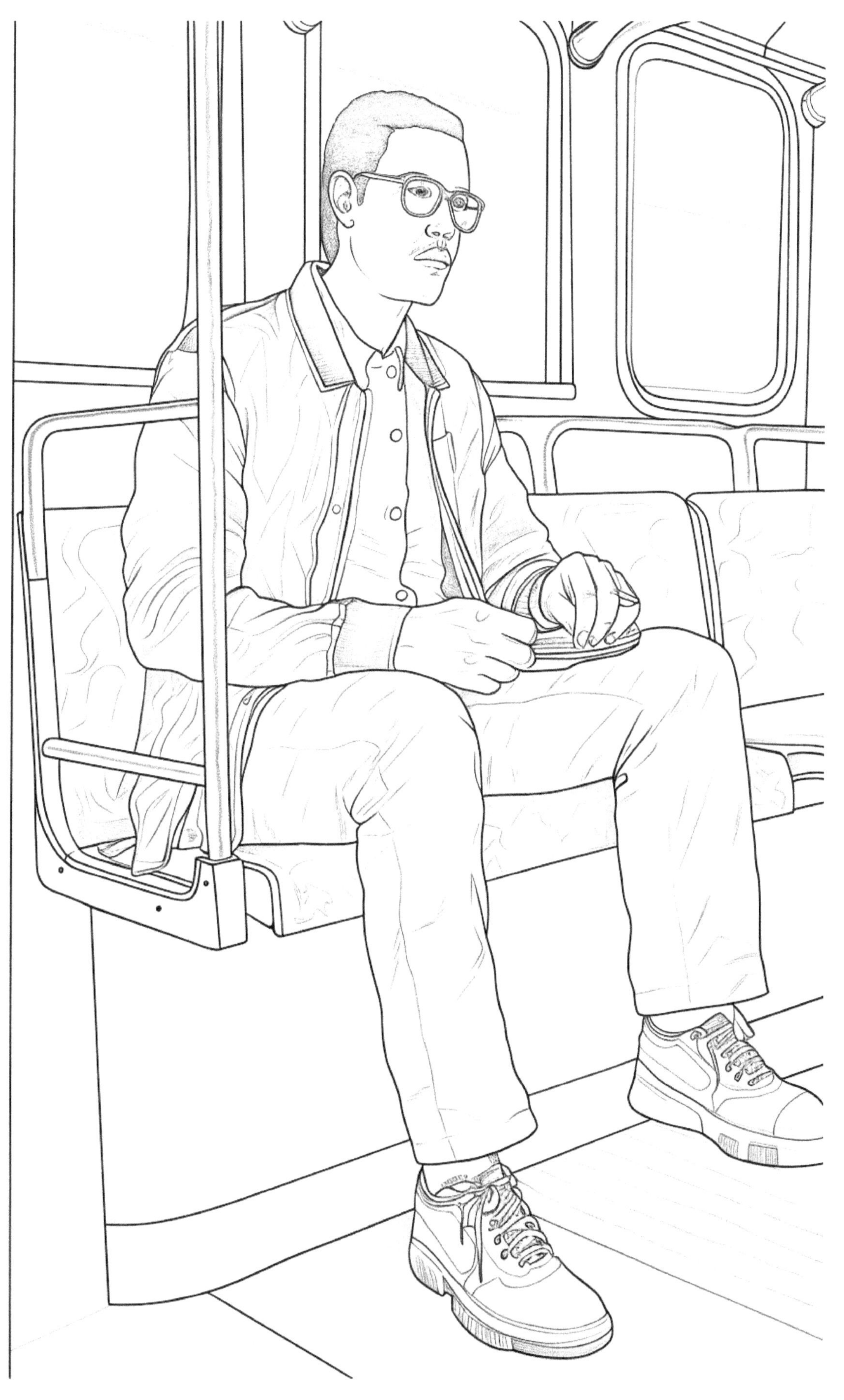

Doctor's wise counsel

Fiber rich foods must be had

Healthy gut awaits

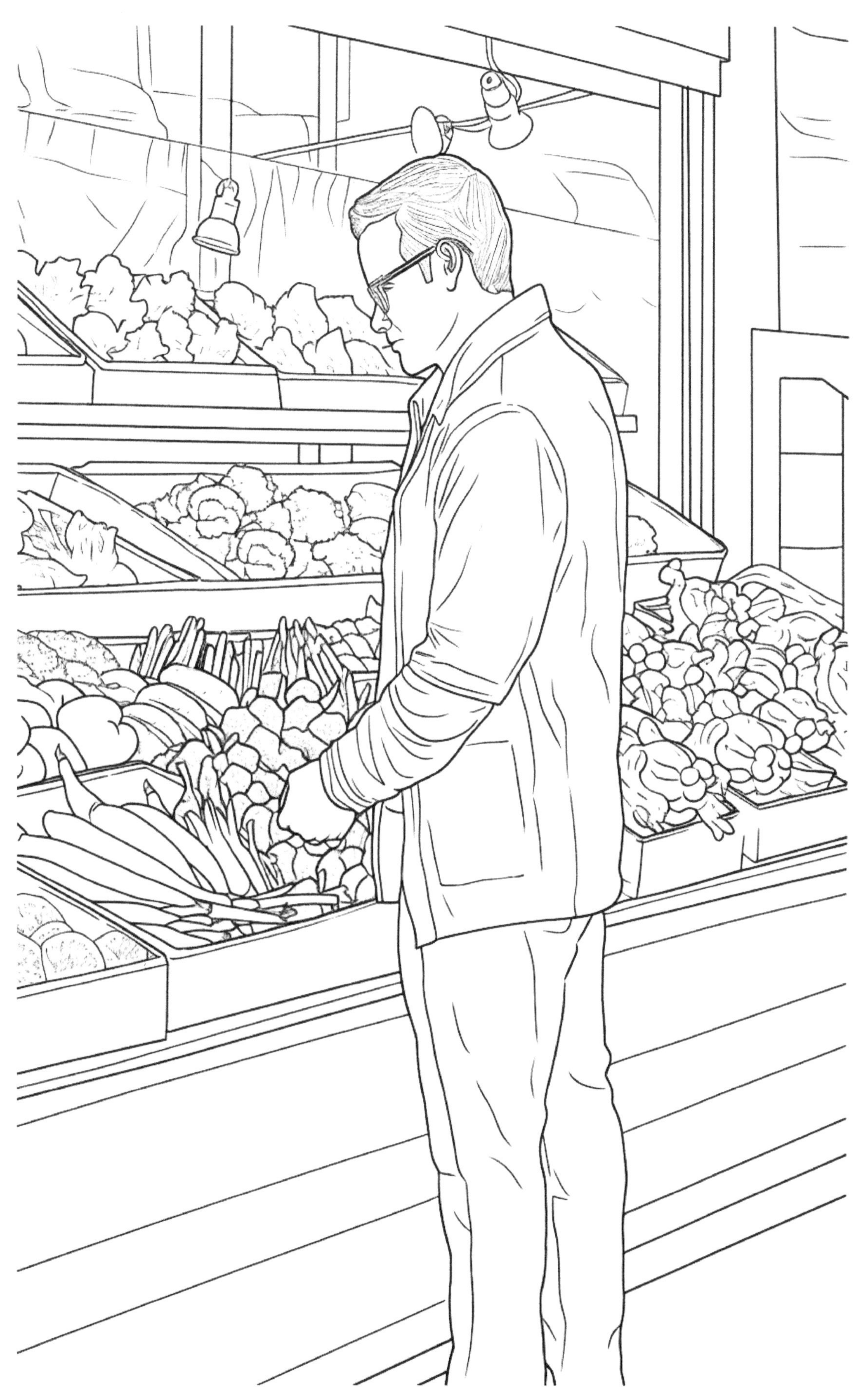

Water in my bag

TSA confiscated

Now I am thirsty

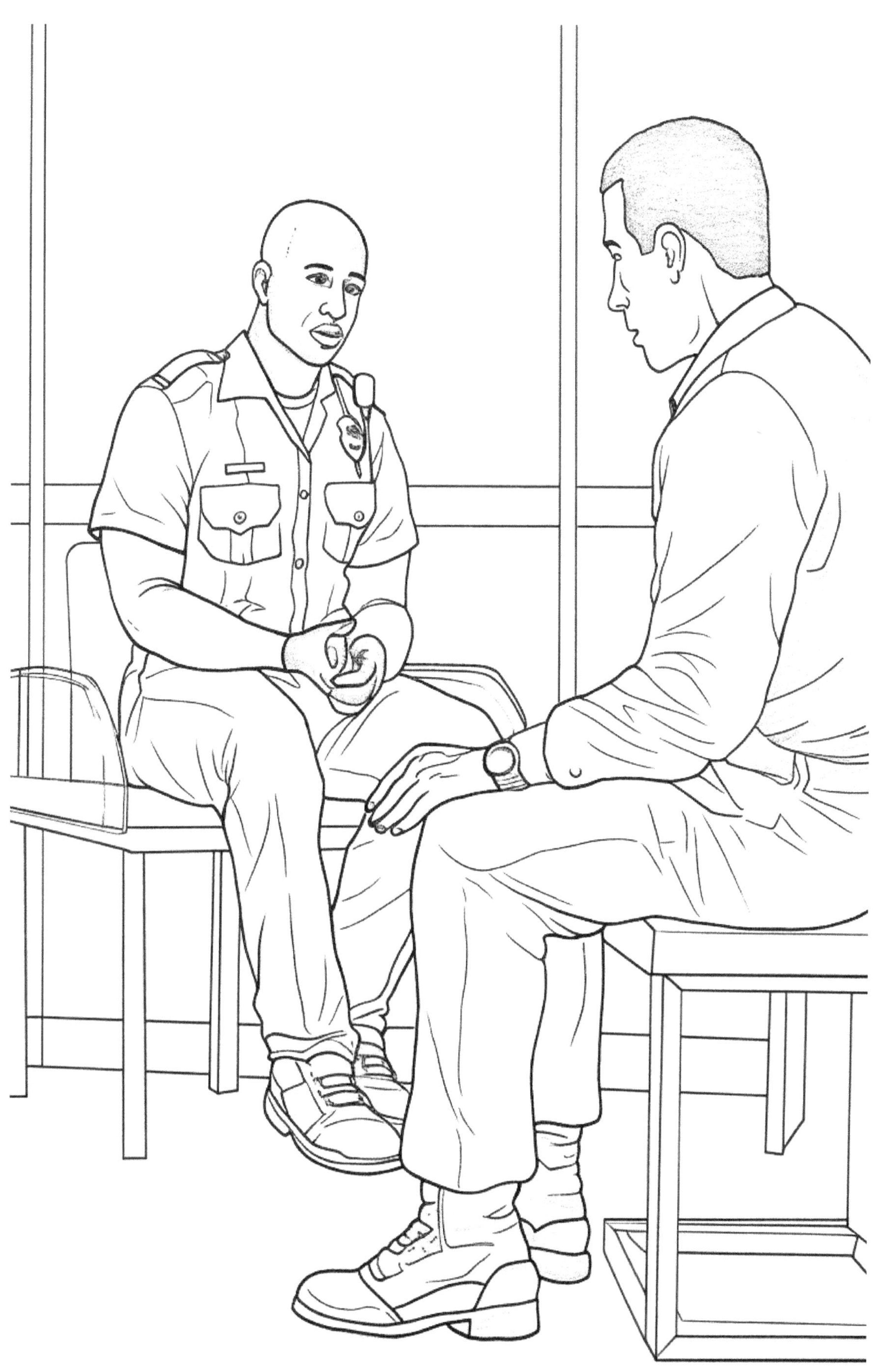

Paying bills again

I'd rather buy a new toy

But I'm broke, so no

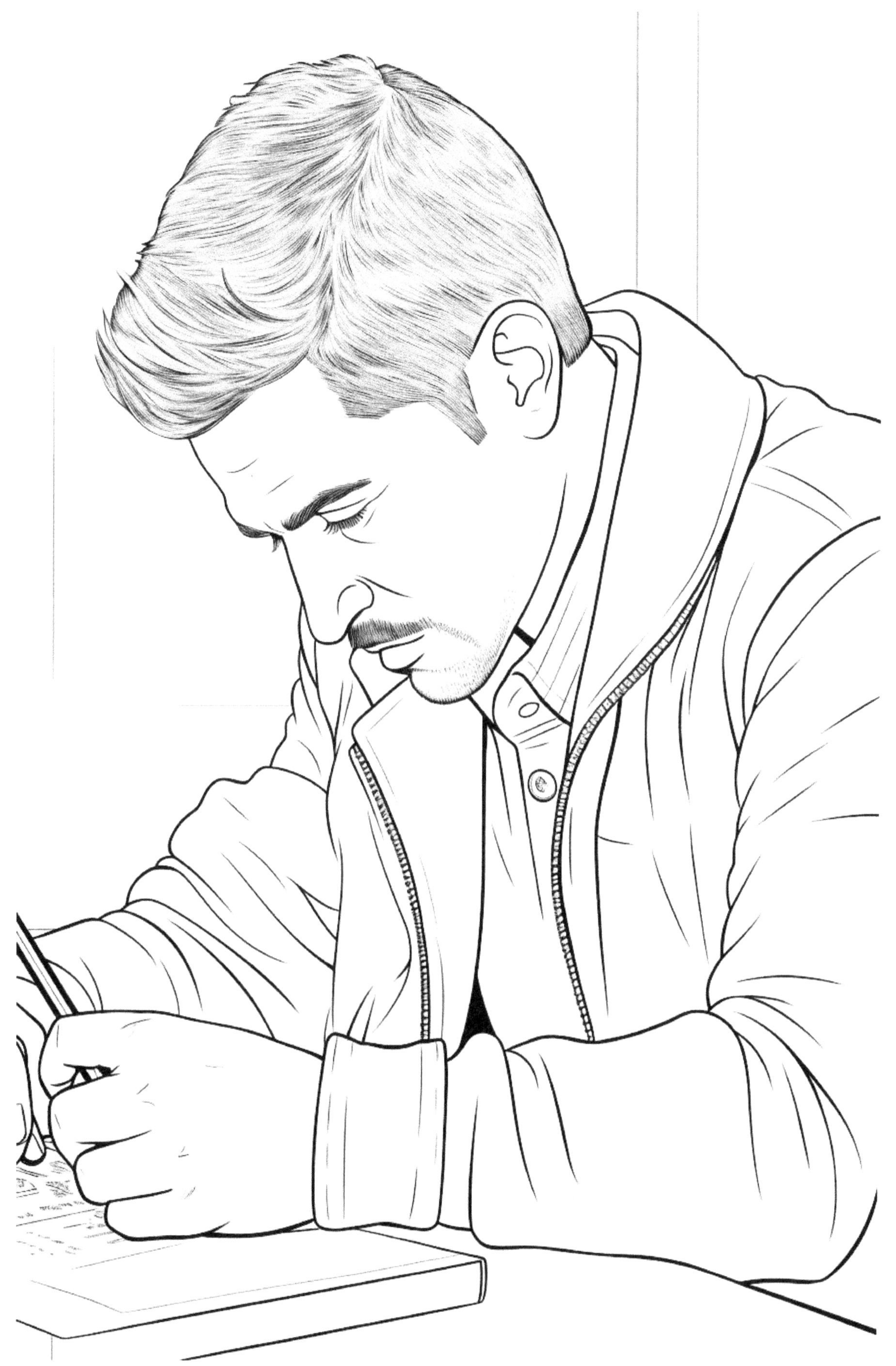

Where's my car? Not sure

I will just wander around

Pretending I know

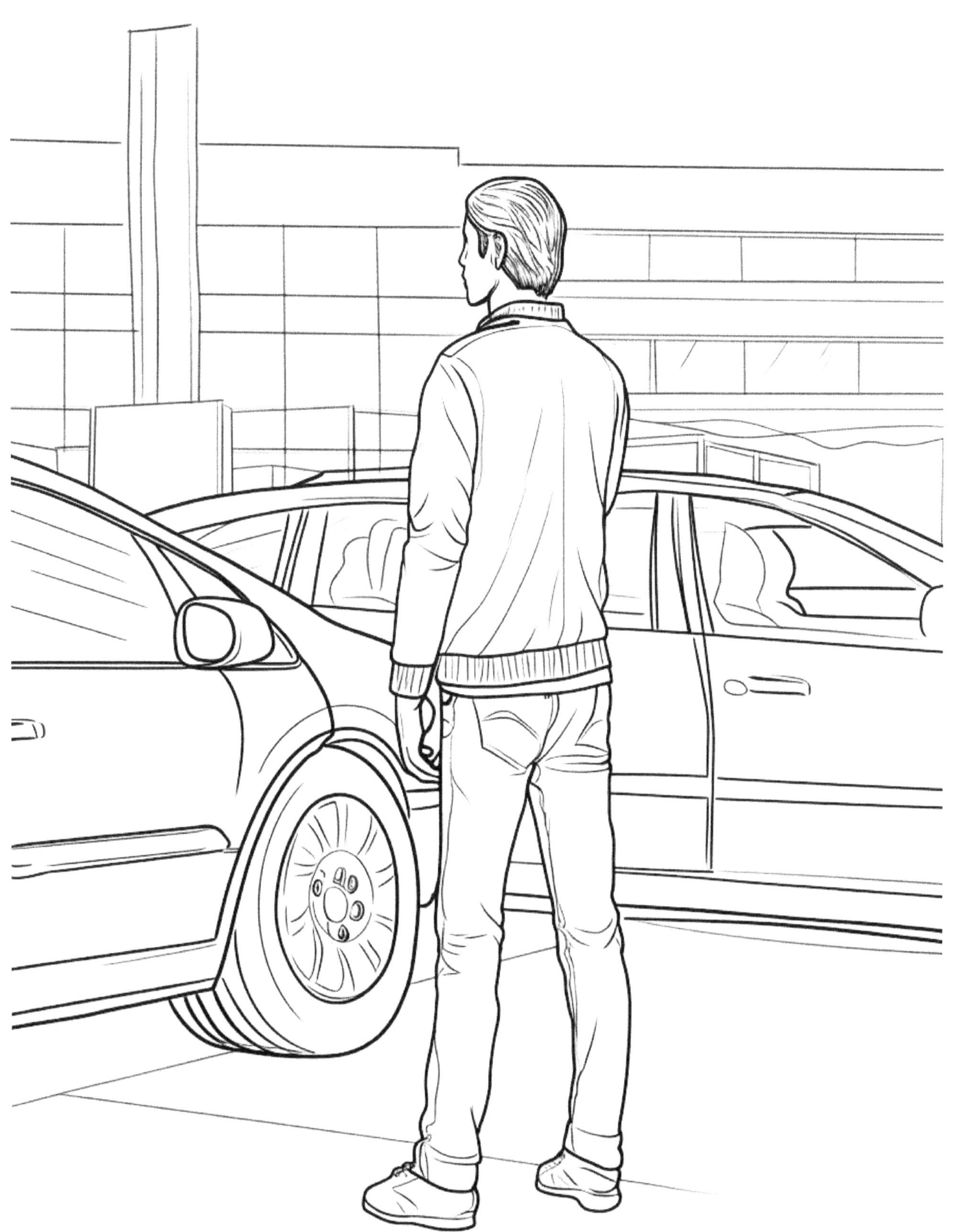

Sitting on a bench

I could people-watch all day

Are they watching me?

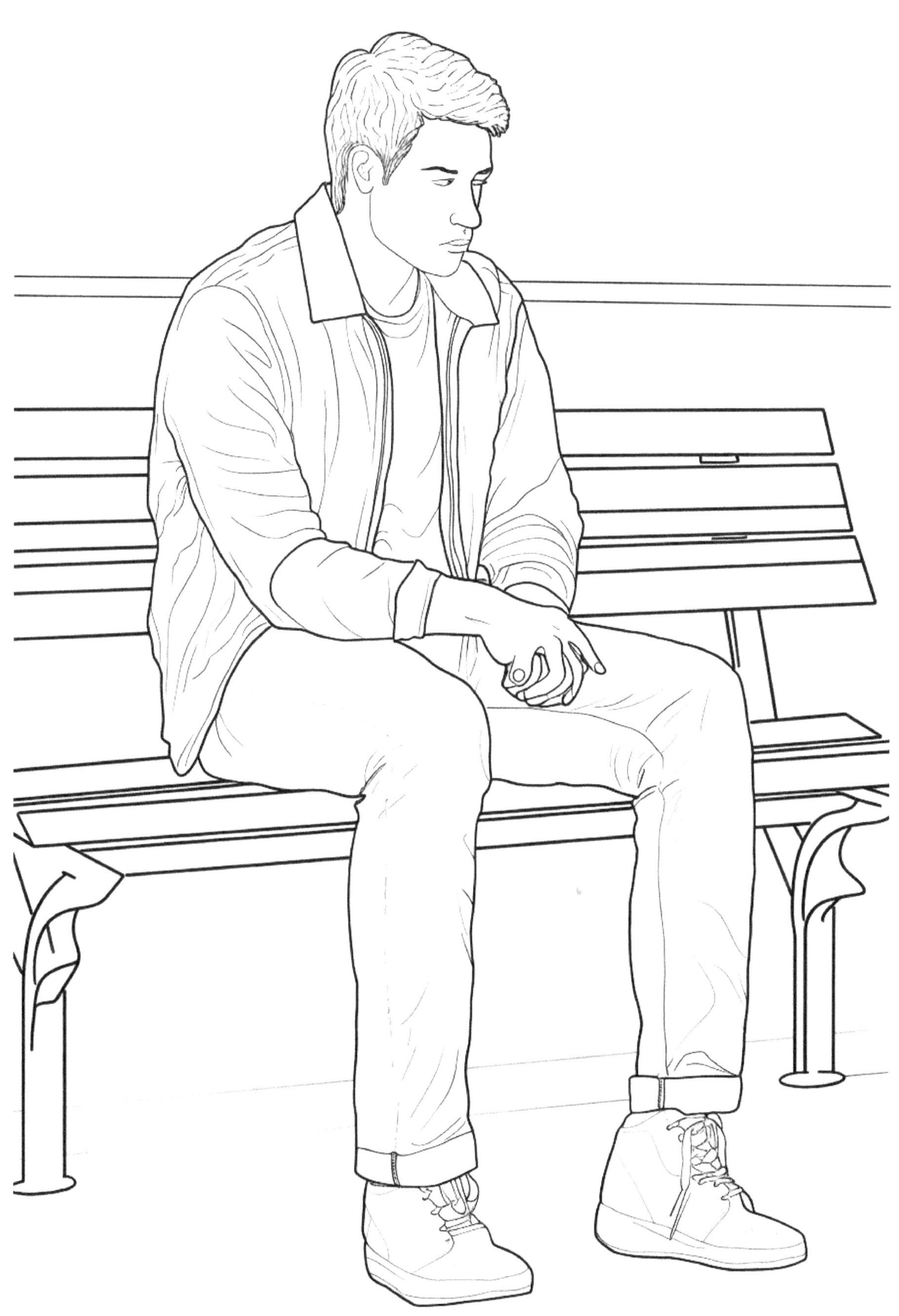

Everything, one bag

I should have double bagged it

Hope it doesn’t break

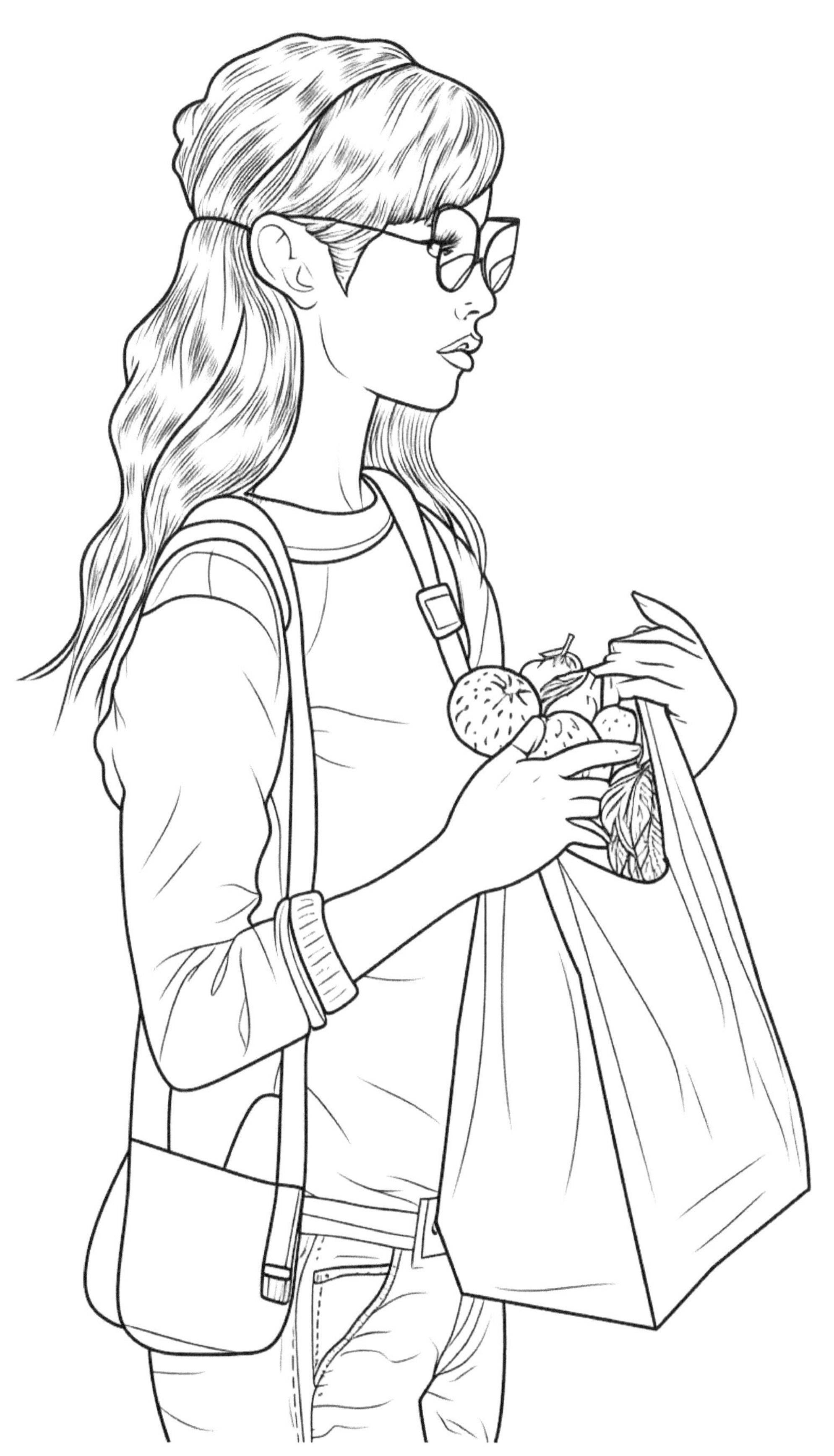

I'm mowing the lawn

A Zen-like experience

Until the bee stings

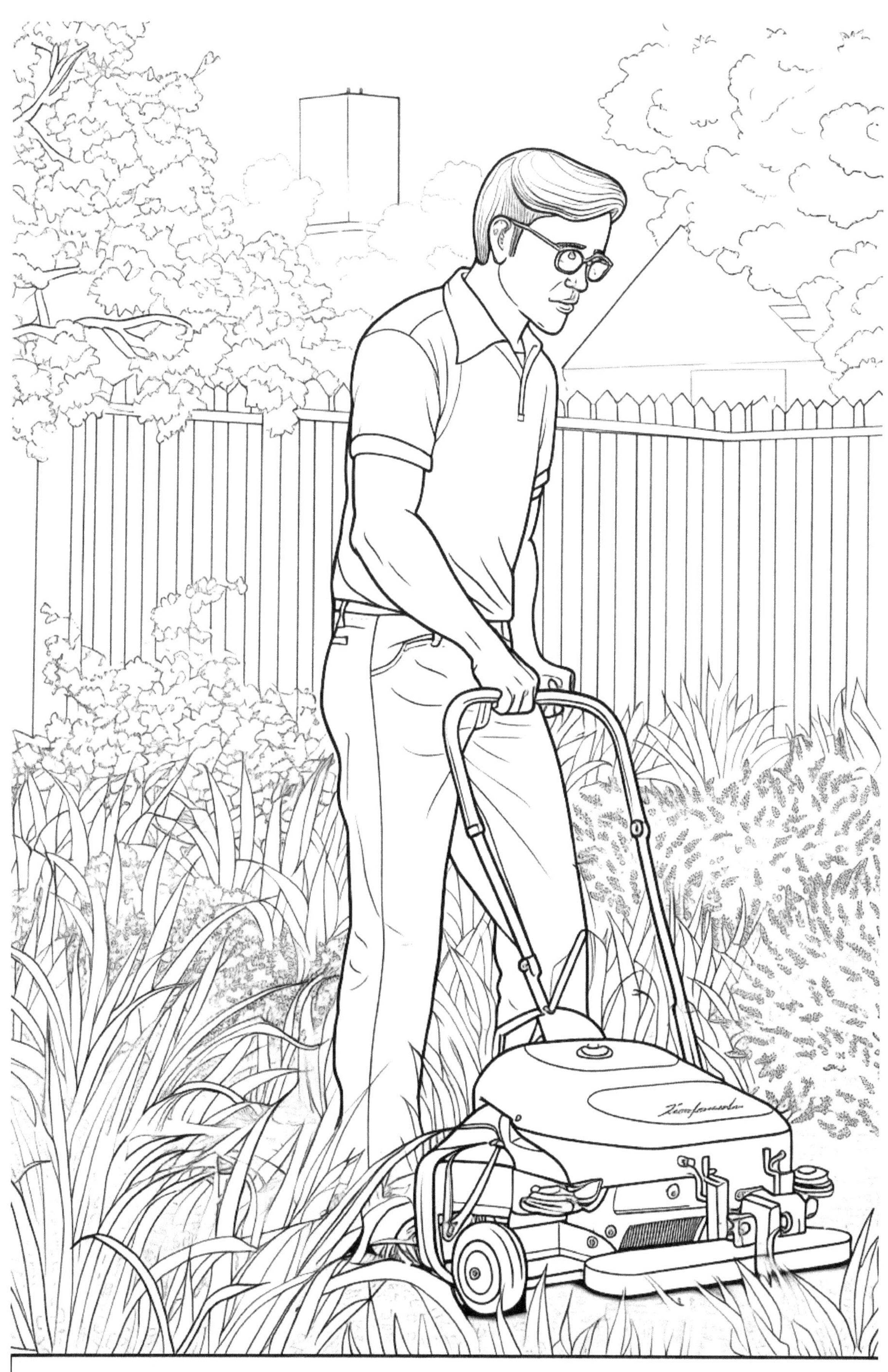

Matinee movie

All alone, I laugh and cry

I need more popcorn

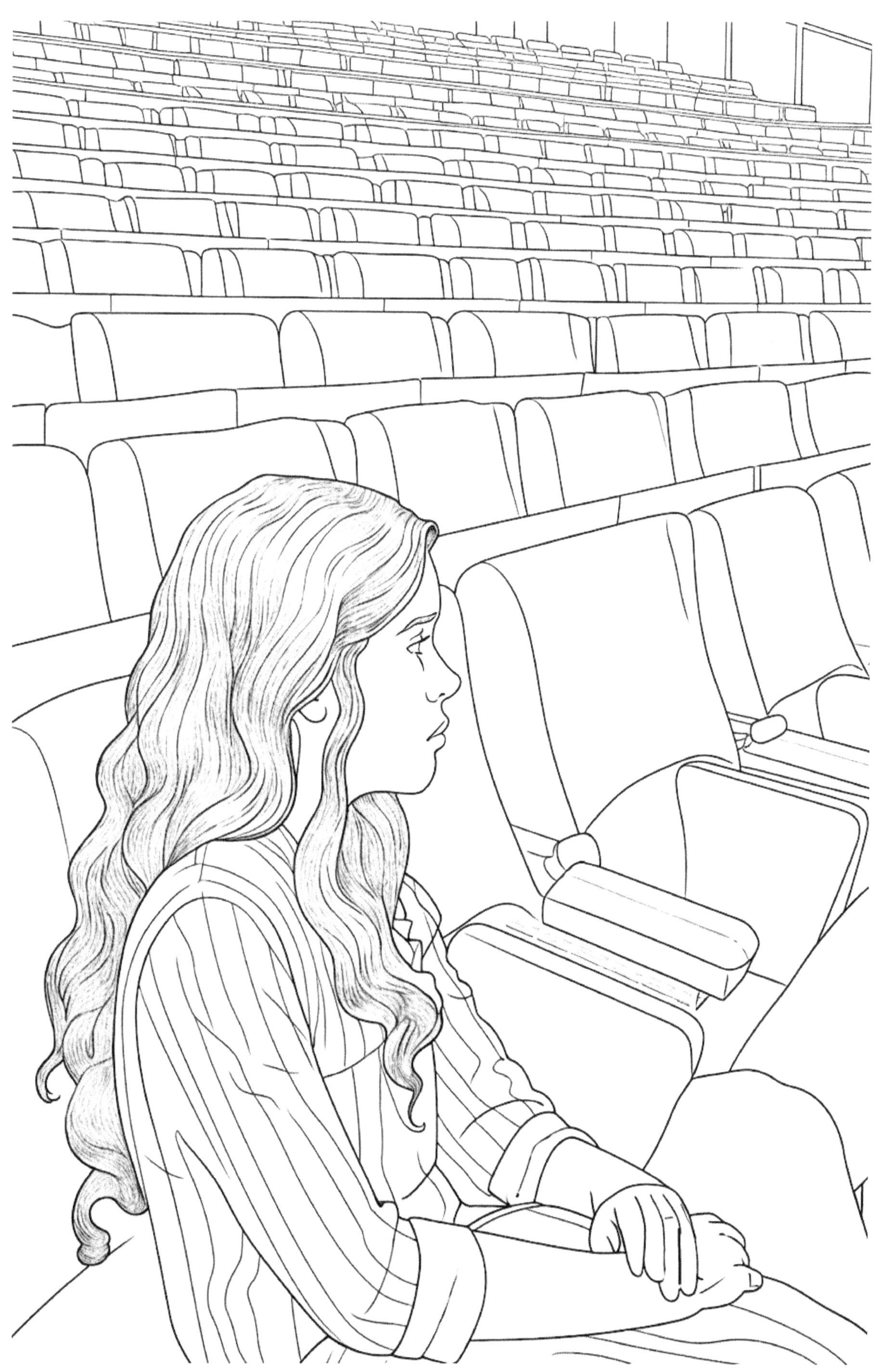

Clouds are like a game

I spot shapes, make up stories

The day passes by

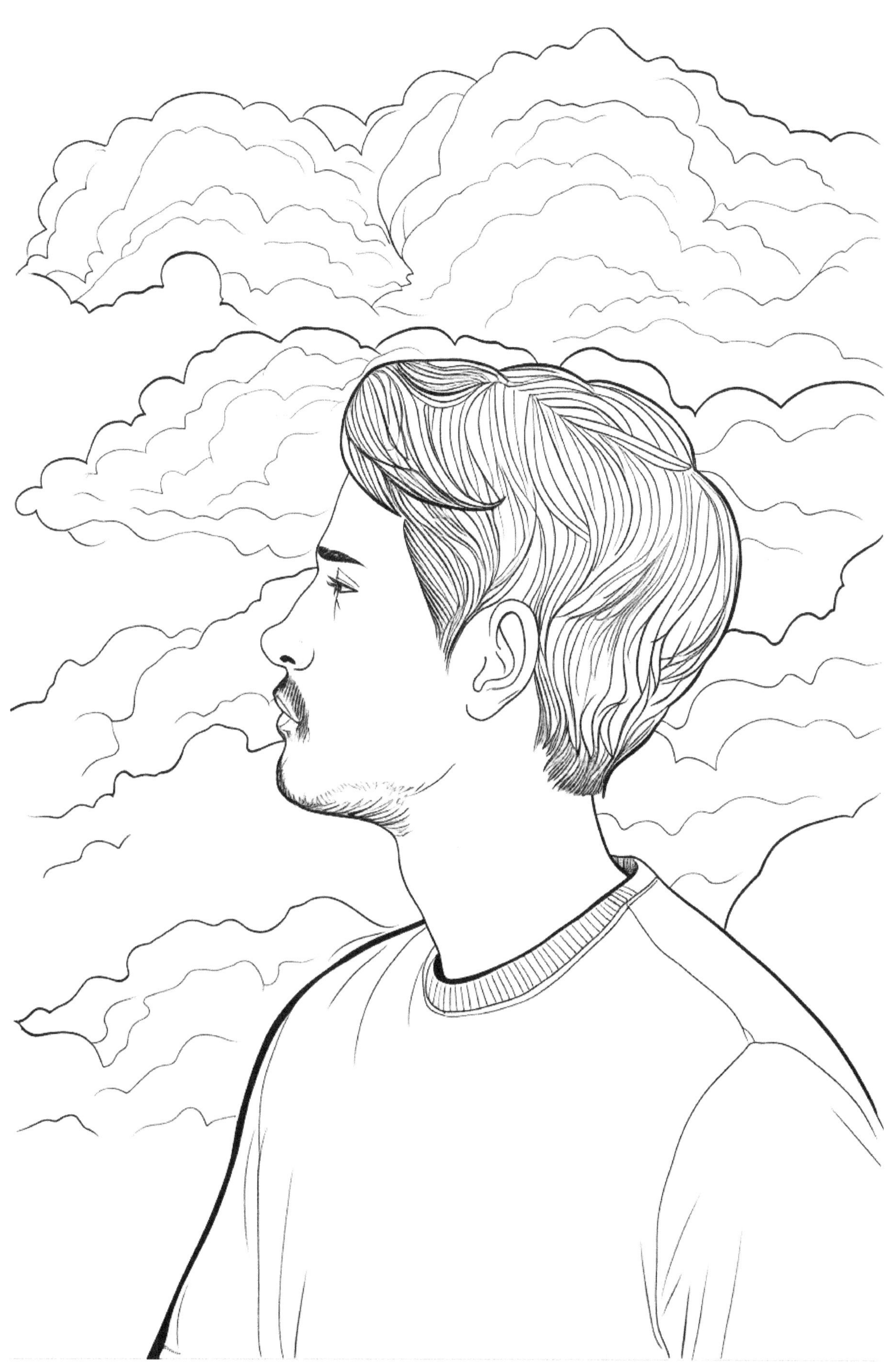

Winter tree hugging

A cold embrace, but I'm warm

From the inside out

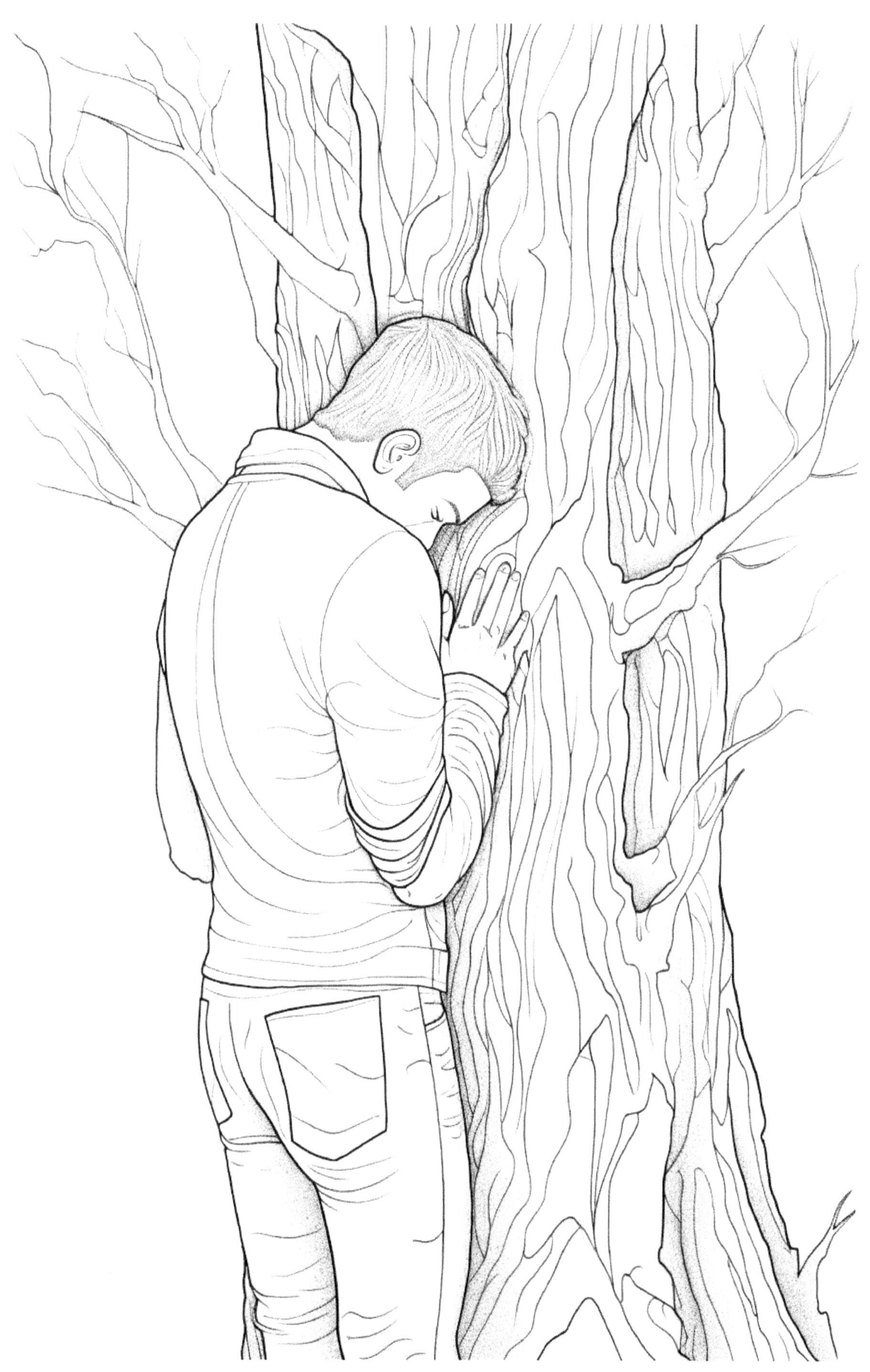

My house is burning

I hope insurance covers

The cost of my socks

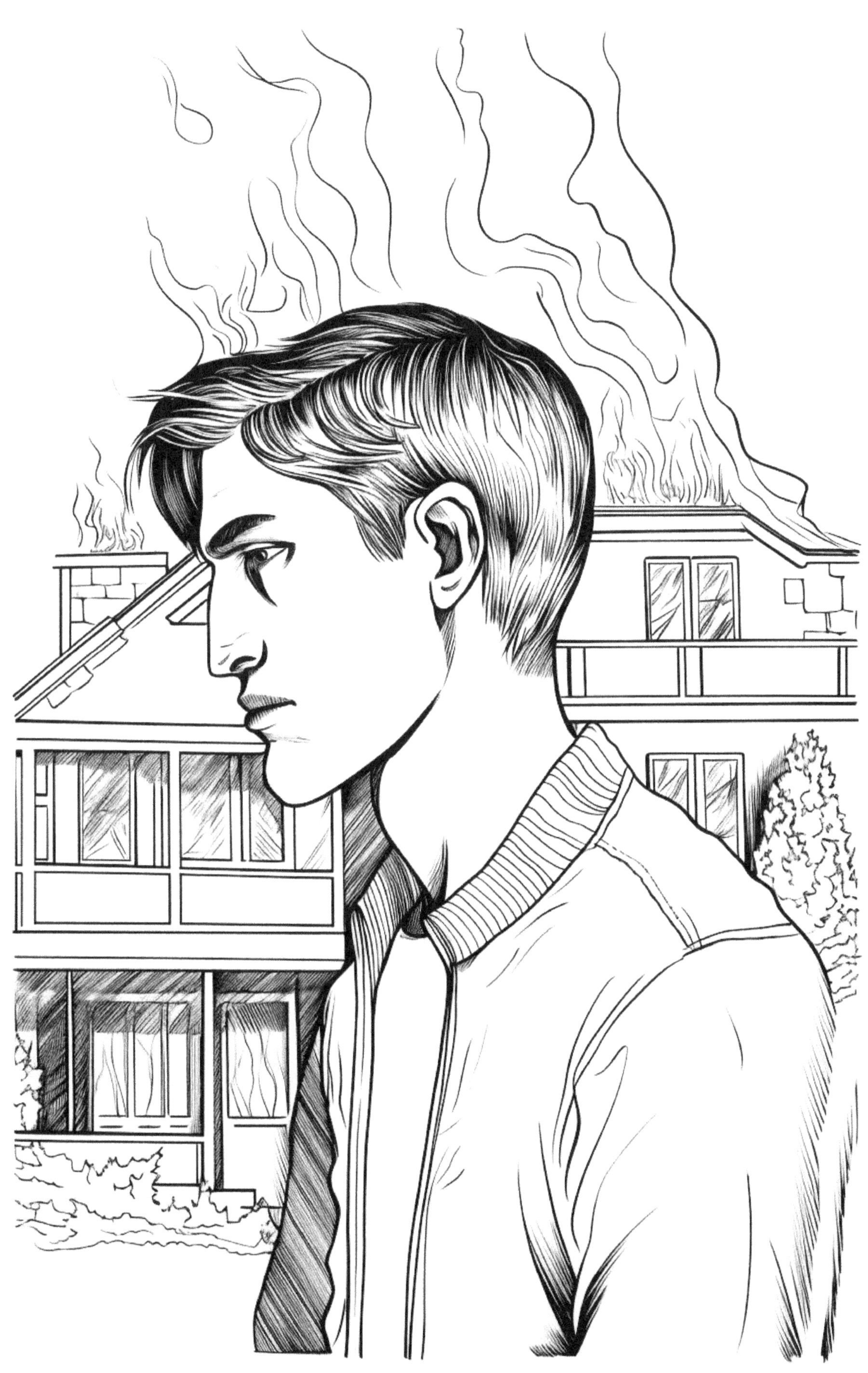

Grocery shopping

I go in for milk and bread

And come out with cake

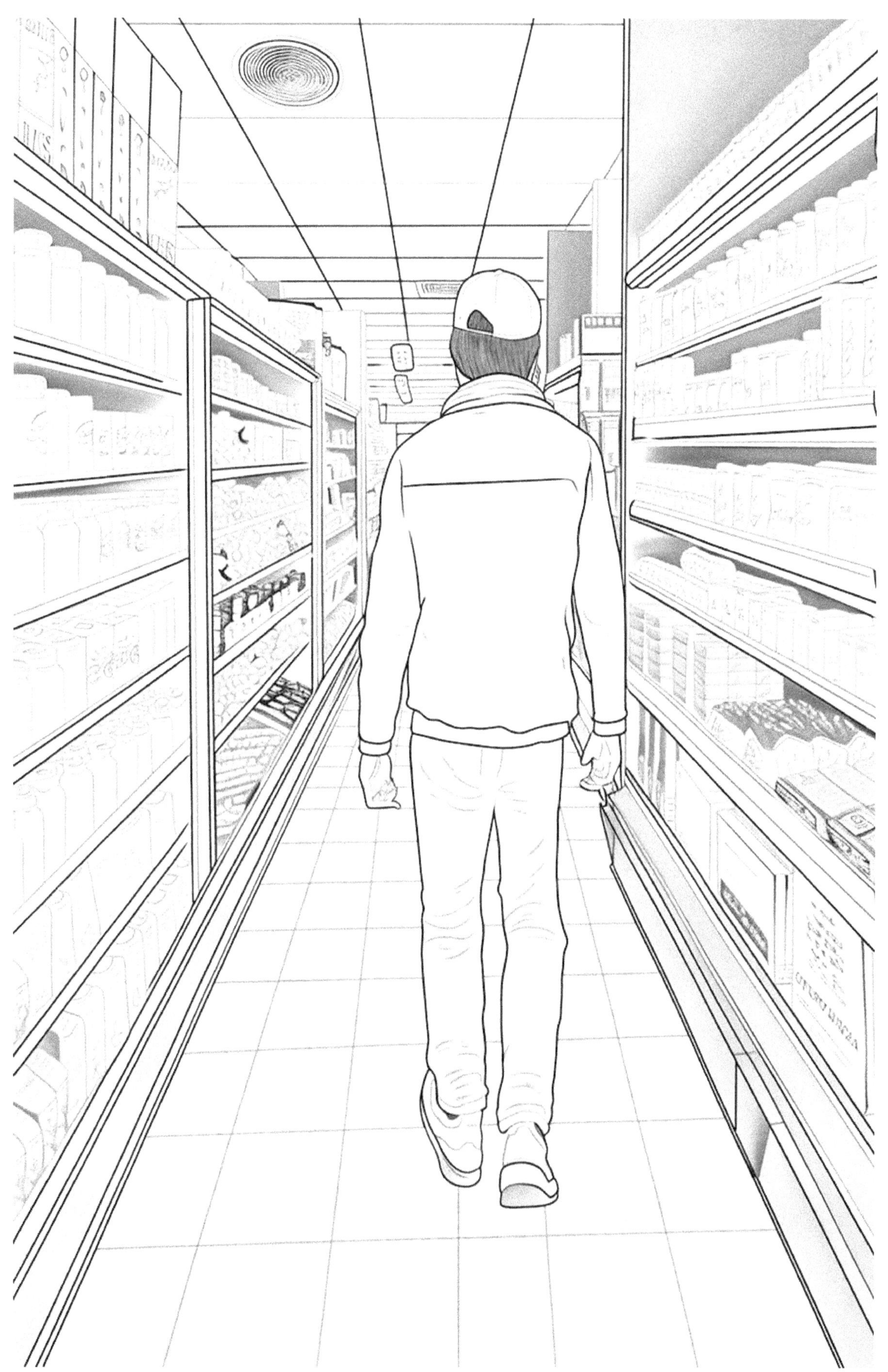

Phone always in hand

I've forgotten how to use

A pencil, it seems

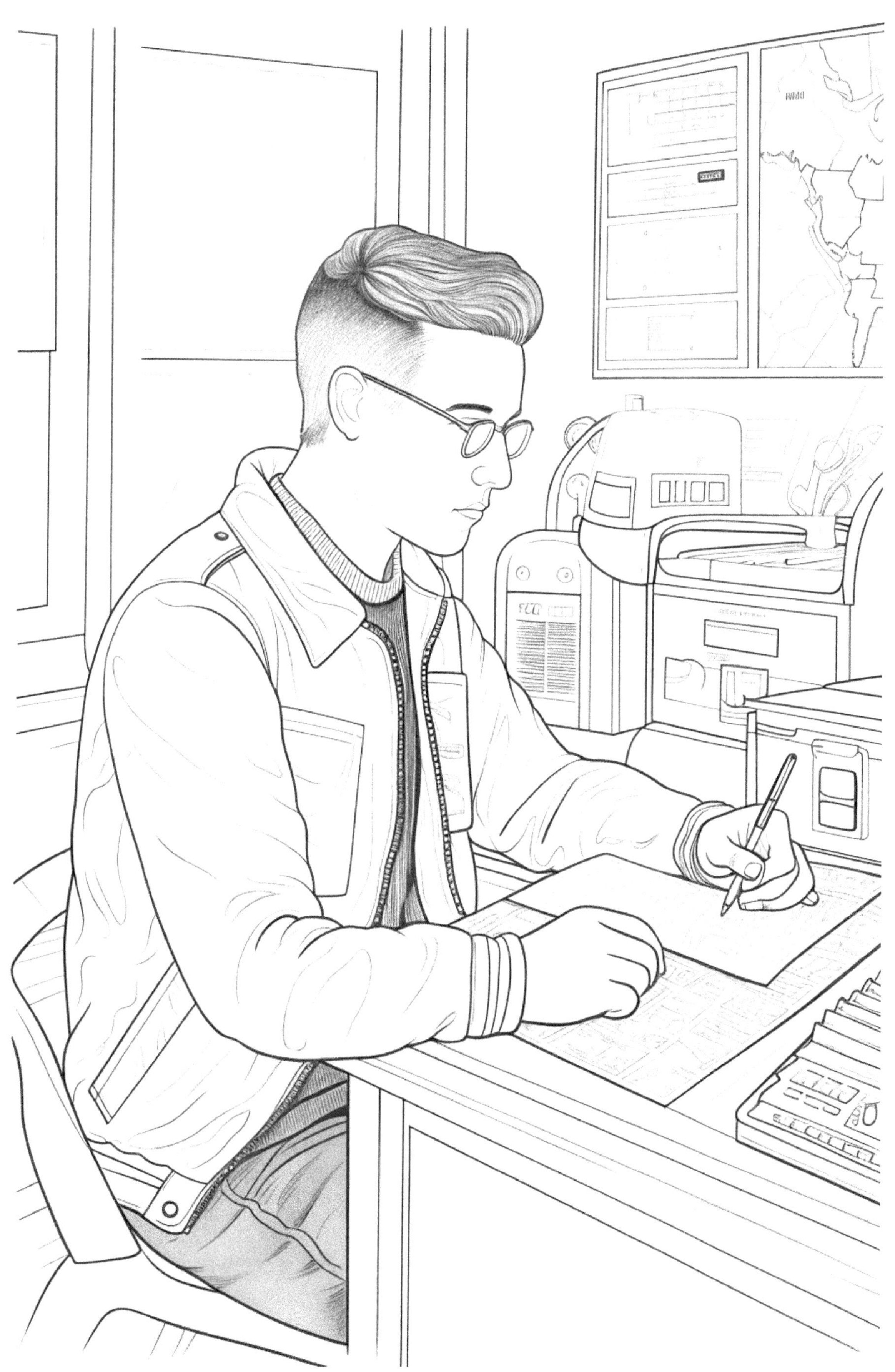

A tiny sandwich

Just a few bites and it's gone

I am still hungry

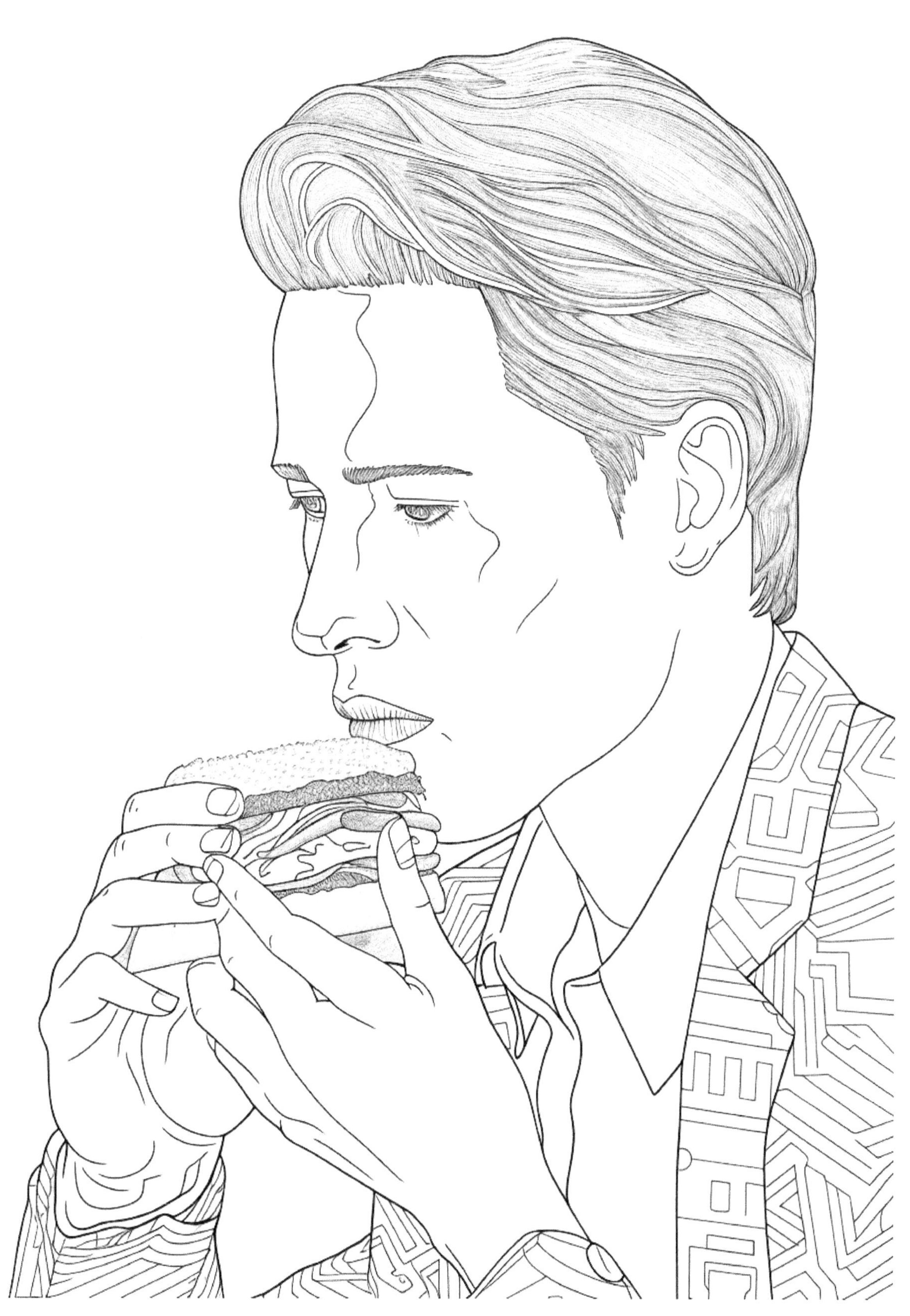

Pasta in my mouth

Spaghetti, penne and more

I eat the noodles

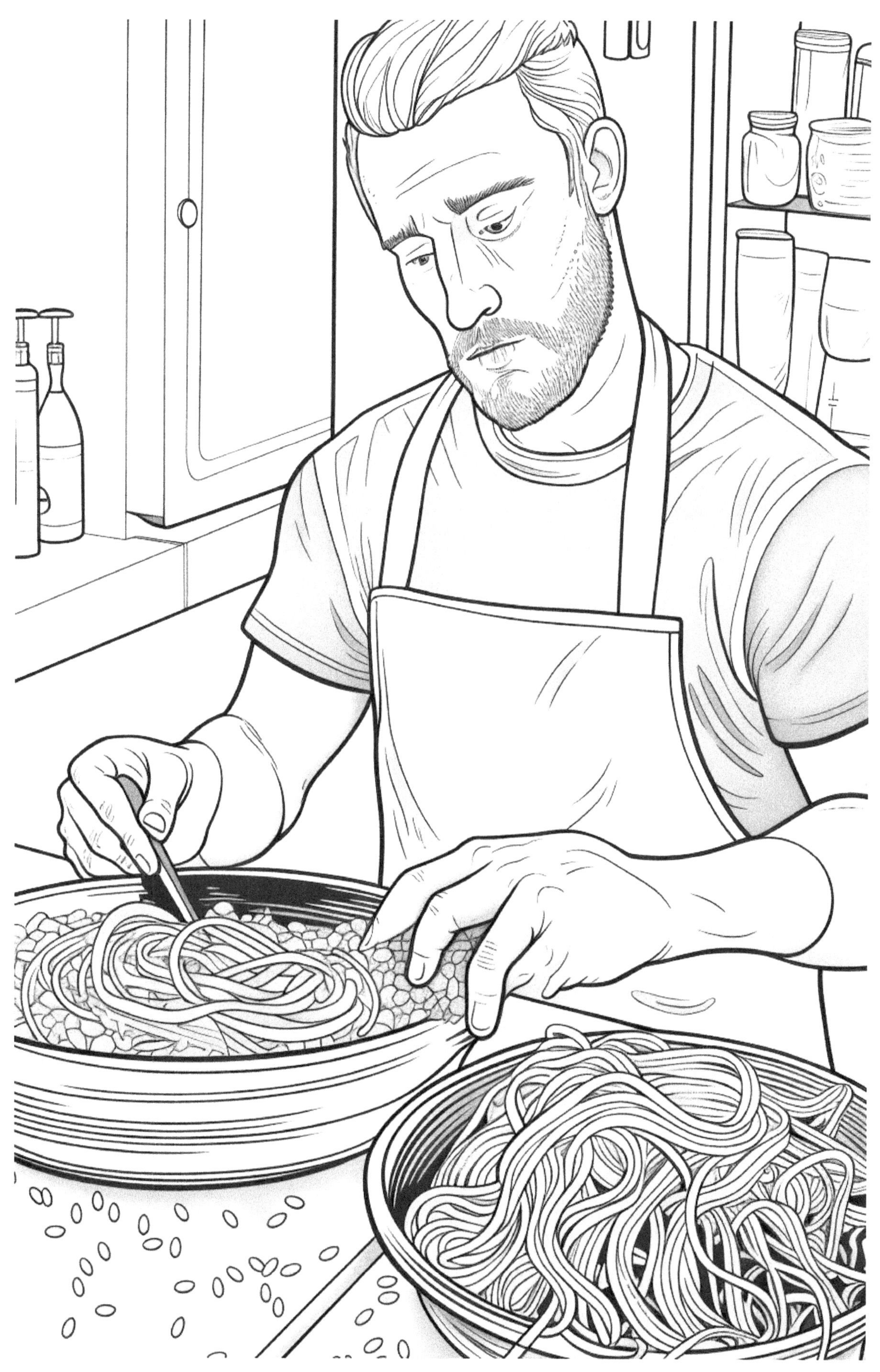

Dishes piled high

I scrub and rinse and repeat

Never-ending chore

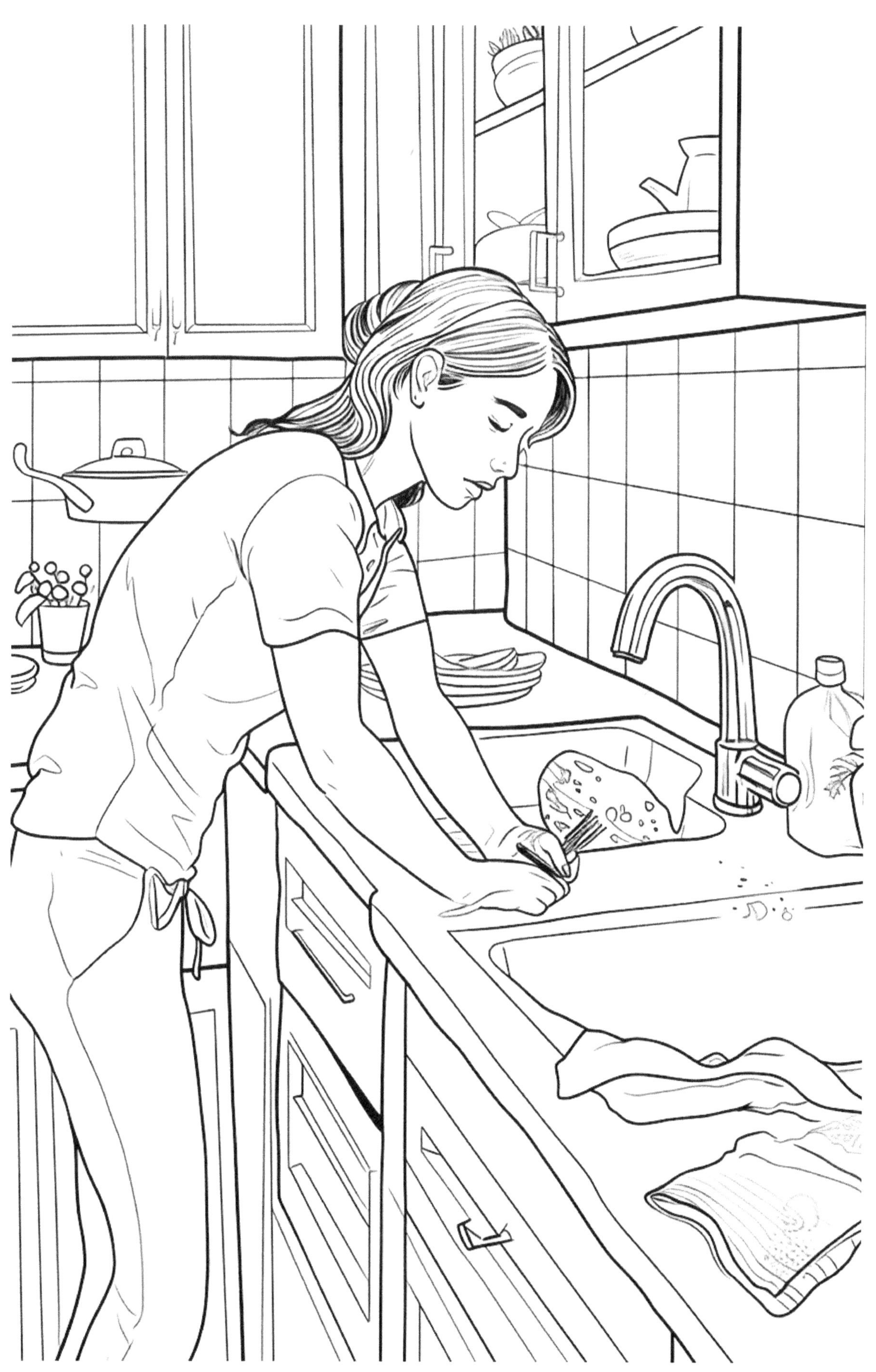

Couch naps are the best

Snuggle with my throw blanket

And dream of pizza

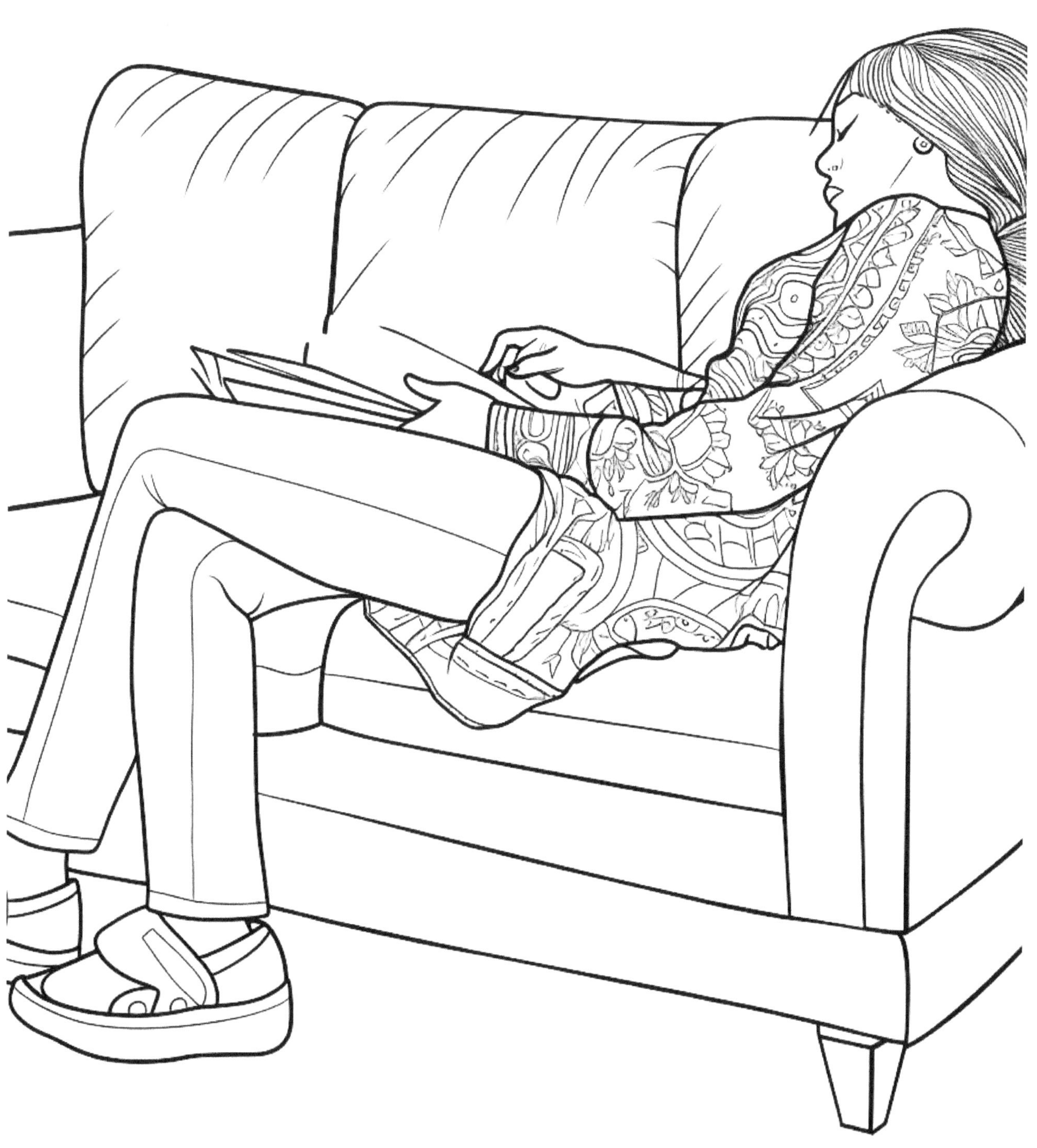

Pre-made cookie dough

The lazy baker's delight

Ain't got time for scratch

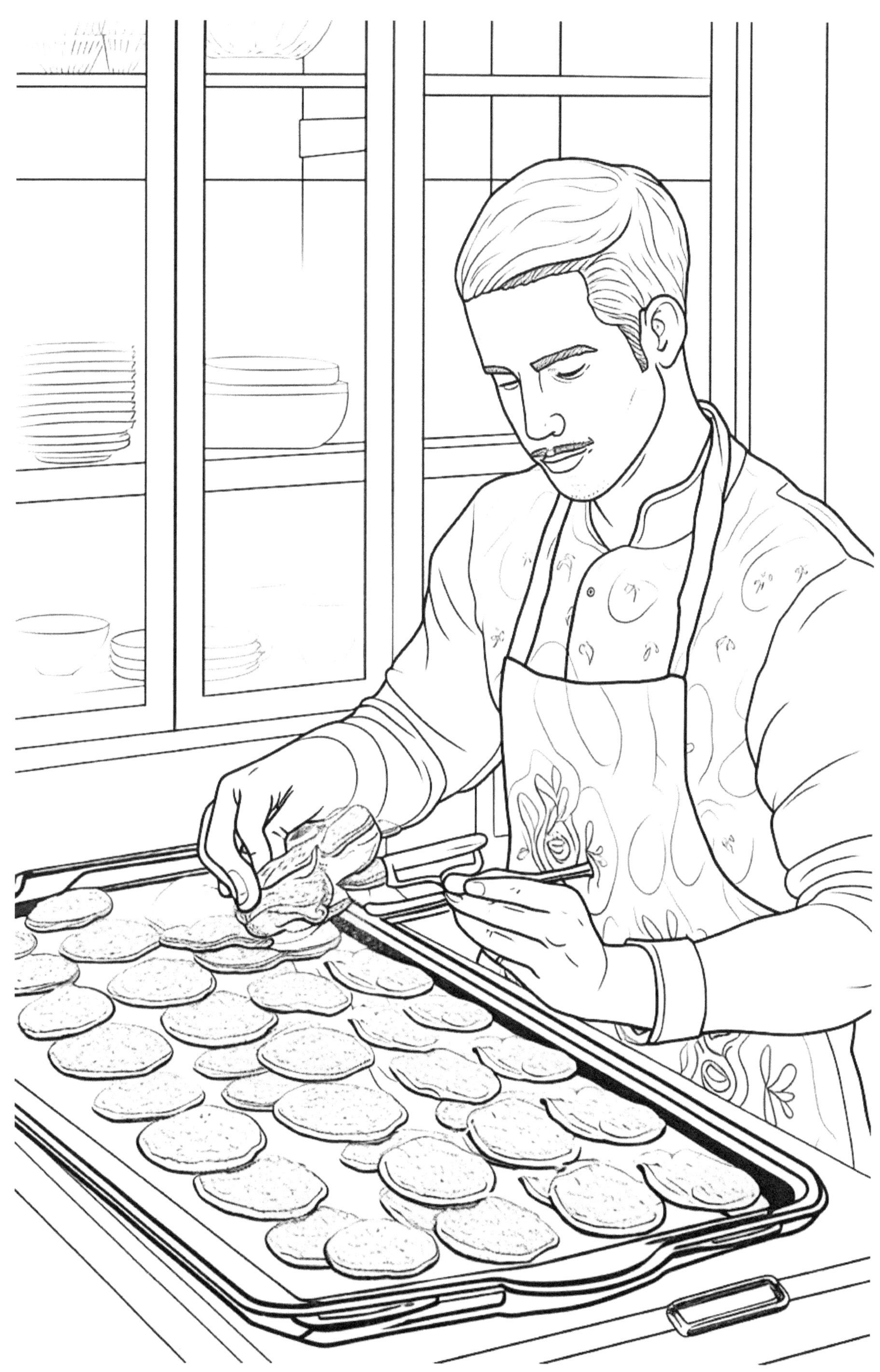

Roman numerals

A puzzle to solve, I see

I'll just Google it

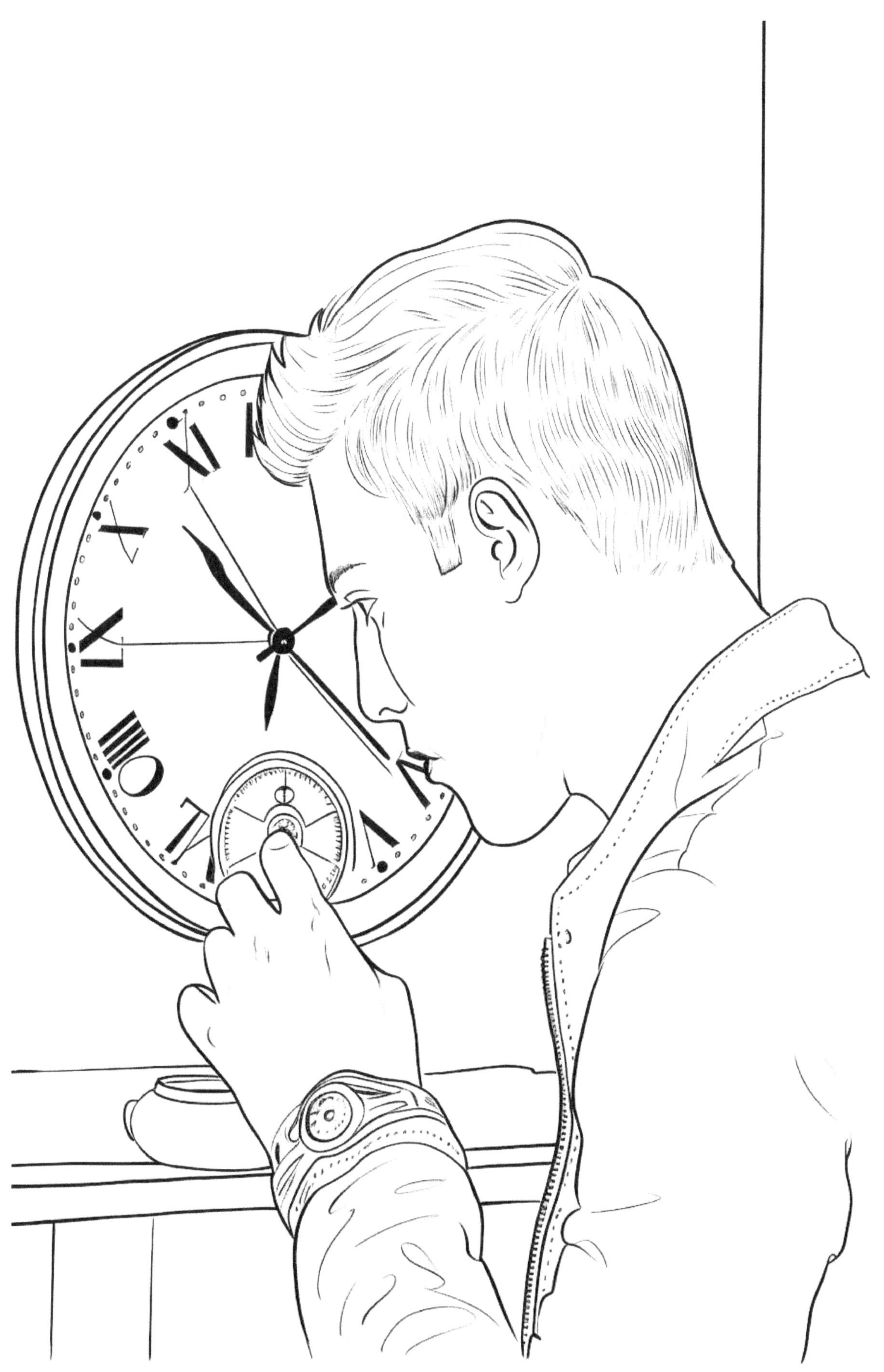

www.ingramcontent.com/pod-product-compliance
Lightning Source LLC
LaVergne TN
LVHW081421110826
845149LV00010B/1827

9781961062009